FEAR IS A LIAR!

ONWARD and UPWARD,

PRAISE FOR

REIMAGINING BLUE

"Kristen Ziman's *Reimagining Blue* is a compelling story of one woman's passion for the police profession. In vivid and personal detail she tells of her inspiring journey from a teenage cadet to police chief of Aurora, Illinois, where she faced her greatest challenge: responding to Illinois's worst mass shooting.

There are eighteen thousand police chiefs in the United States. Fewer than five hundred are women. Kristen helped smash the glass ceiling that held so many women back in the profession. After reading this book, you'll understand how she achieved a career of significance in her chosen profession."

BILL BRATTON
Former New York City police commissioner

"Kristen Ziman beautifully captures the emotional gamut in this powerful masterpiece. She isn't afraid to detail her personal journey from a teen cadet to overseeing the response to Illinois's worst mass shooting in her own city. *Reimagining Blue* underscores the importance and significance of law enforcement officials and first responders while acknowledging the room for growth and improvement. With encouragement, positive reinforcement, and tough love, Kristen shows us all how to enact meaningful change through the mantra 'Be Better.' This book is just a 'next step' in Kristen's journey . . . I know she will continue to change the world. Kristen is a powerful female role model who inspires everyone."

ANDREA DARLAS
Chicago news anchor and reporter, WGN-TV

"Chief Ziman gives us an unflinching view into modern policing. Her story is unexpectedly riveting, and will undoubtedly shine a light for those wanting to know more about the human behind the badge."

SYLVIA MOIR
Former police chief of El Cerrito, California, and Tempe, Arizona

"Chief Kristen Ziman has written a clear, compelling, and challenging book. As the daughter of a cop and a leader of cops, she is helping America make a positive difference."

REV. DR. DERWIN L. GRAY
Author of *How to Heal the Racial Divide*

REIMAGINING
BLUE

www.amplifypublishing.com

Reimagining Blue: Thoughts on Life, Leadership, and a New Way Forward in Policing

The author has tried to recreate events, locales, and conversations from their memories of them. In order to maintain their anonymity in some instances they may have changed the names of individuals and places. They may have changed some identifying characteristics and details.

For more information, please contact Amplify Publishing
620 Herndon Parkway #320
Herndon, VA 20170
info@amplifypublishing.com

Library of Congress Control Number: 2021921768

CPSIA Code: PRV0122A
ISBN-13: 978-1-63755-125-7

Printed in the United States

Dedicated to the noble police officers across the globe who are aligned to purpose and service. You continue to inspire me with your selflessness and bravery. I have tremendous faith that our profession will continue to improve—not because it's broken, but because we must always be better. And to the men and women of the Aurora Police Department, both past and present. You are my muse and my inspiration.

REIMAGINING BLUE

THOUGHTS ON LIFE, LEADERSHIP, AND A NEW WAY FORWARD IN POLICING

FORMER
POLICE CHIEF **KRISTEN ZIMAN**

CONTENTS

INTRODUCTION

I woke up on June 1, 2020, and for the first time in my twenty-seven-year career, I questioned whether I wanted to be a cop anymore. I have had peaks and valleys throughout my professional life, but even on the worst days, I never considered leaving. June 1 was the day after the riots that erupted all over the nation in response to the murder of George Floyd, and I drove around my city assessing the aftermath. Our businesses were looted and burned. Remnants of broken glass from the windows that were smashed littered the streets. Bricks that were pried up from the sidewalks and thrown at our officers were scattered all over the downtown. The scene looked like war.

I suppose it was war. Derek Chauvin's knee on the neck of George Floyd caused the nation to bubble over in anger and emotion and declare war on the entire police institution. My first reaction was that of defensiveness. Chauvin did not represent the best of law enforcement, and I couldn't understand why the rest of us were being punished for his transgression. Aurora is the second largest city in the state of Illinois, and our officers weren't making negative headlines. Our officers have worked diligently to build relationships in our community. Our officers have been trained to a standard of conduct that places value on human life and de-escalation. But none of that mattered because in a flip of a switch, we became the common enemy.

I've worn a police uniform since I was twenty-one, and each day that I have pinned my police star onto my chest, I have felt proud. I've always loved the feeling I get when I walk out into the world in my uniform. I stand up a little taller because I feel fearless and confident with my arm patches flanking my shoulders and my rank insignia displayed on my collar. I feel powerful but not the kind of power *over* another. I feel the kind of power that affords me the authority to protect people from bullies. I have the power to take evildoers into custody and strip them of their freedom so they can't harm their victims anymore. Even though I'm small in stature, people listen to me because of the uniform. I have used my power for good, and as I look back on my career, I can say that I have never abused my position or my badge. I have wanted to be a police officer my entire life, and I have loved every moment of it.

When I started as a police cadet in 1991, the Rodney King incident had just occurred, so it was my first indoctrination to unrest. It didn't compare to George Floyd, but even as a wide-eyed seventeen-year-old, I understood that police action could send a ripple effect across the nation. Every negative action by a police officer results in all of us being painted with a broad brush. I remember hanging out at the front desk of the police department listening to the cops talk about Rodney King. At that time, it was accepted practice to give a person who fled from the police a "what for" as a result of the effort involved in chasing them. Whether it be a foot pursuit or a vehicle pursuit, I was told by a veteran cop that running away gets the offender a few blows once you had them in custody. This was what it was like in the '90s in policing. The cops seemed to downplay the incident despite the riots that were occurring. Maybe they were unaffected because the rioting was relegated mostly to the LA area. Or maybe I wasn't paying close enough attention to the national policing stage at that time. I was so focused on my corner of the world, and I was so happy to be working at the police department, and I believed everything the officers told me. I remember hearing several members of the public talk about Rodney King. "That's what happens when you run from the police." When I watched the video of King, I fell in line with what the cops were saying. It wasn't racial in my mind. I don't care who you are; you don't run from the police. As I look back on that incident now, I see it *far* differently. It's a clear and undeniable act of excessive force. I was seventeen years old and was consistently told by my cop dad and my cop colleagues that you don't question authority, so it felt accepted to impose consequences when it occurred. For context, that was also the era of corporal punishment. I got paddled at school, and I got the belt at home. I shudder at those practices present day, but back then, leaving welts on a child's behind wasn't considered child abuse as it is now. Cops weren't the enemy for the most part, and there wasn't a crisis in policing like there is now. And policing evolved over the years for the better. In my own midsized department, I saw a formal police accountability division emerge. Policies became more stringent surrounding the use of force. Squad cameras were installed to record officers' actions. Community policing was adopted, and we were trained to engage our residents. More women and minorities joined our ranks. Our profession got more professional, and I saw it happen with my own eyes.

Rodney King and George Floyd are bookends to my career, and now I'm questioning my own sanity because it feels like the rest of the world didn't see us get better. But we did get better, and I am here to convince you of that.

I have been at my police department in Aurora, Illinois, for thirty years. I still chose to be a cop despite the LA riots after the Rodney King incident in 1991. Through the unrest in Ferguson, Missouri, in 2014. Through a 2019 mass shooting in my own city, when I witnessed the good my officers could do. Despite all the negative headlines, I believe in policing when our officers are at their best, but I am struggling with the things that happen when we are at our worst. And I'm struggling with the hatred toward police because it's not fair to the great cops who are aligned with the law and serve their communities selflessly. I worked my way up through the ranks in my department to become the first female lieutenant, commander, and chief, and this book chronicles my life in law enforcement and my personal struggles with my profession and myself. As you will learn, I have strong feelings about various issues of the day, especially as they relate to policing, but in order to understand my opinions, you need to understand who I am and where I come from. These musings are a compilation of my childhood and personal experiences intertwined with my professional life. This book is an anthology of my trek through leadership and life. It is not arranged in chronological order because my stream of consciousness doesn't cooperate in that way. My hope is that by reading this chronicle of my imperfect journey, you will begin to see the vantage point of a person who wears a police uniform. I have found that cops are some of the most misunderstood people, and I hope you walk away with a better understanding of the policing profession from my viewpoint.

I'm a cop, but I'm critical of cops because I don't suffer from the "blind loyalty" affliction that many do. I'm also critical of people who make it their life's work to break the law and harm others and our society, and I believe vehemently that a nation without law enforcers would crumble into chaos and anarchy. These musings will probably upset people on both sides of the issues, and I'm okay with that. I'm not here to make friends. I'm here to offer you a perspective into my world and the complexities of being a cop and a boss of cops. My heart has been cracked open, and what is spilling out might surprise both of us.

CHAPTER ONE

THE UNTHINKABLE

On February 15, 2019, at 1:24 in the afternoon, Commander Keith Cross popped his head in my office and said, "Chief, are you listening to the radio? There's an active shooter." Wait. What? The words hung in the air for a moment until they hit me like a ton of bricks. I remember us falling over each other in the doorway and sprinting down the three flights of stairs until we were in the squad car on the way to the scene. Commander Cross was driving, and Commander Jack Fichtel was in the back seat. We knew from 9-1-1 calls coming in that the shooter was likely a guy who had just been terminated from a manufacturing plant. Jack was the SWAT team commander and was putting on his gear, I was in the front passenger seat hanging onto the "Oh shit" strap, and Keith was driving with lights and siren toward the plant.

I remember hearing Ofc. Russel say over the radio that Ofc. Gomez had just been shot, but they hadn't determined where the shooter was. Moments later, I heard Ofc. Cebulski come over the radio and say he had located four gunshot victims in an office— all presumed dead. As each call came over the radio, Keith, Jack, and I did not speak. Keith focused on getting through the intersections. The next shooting victim was found on a dock. The shooter was on a killing spree, so when the officers started arriving on the scene, he turned his attention to them. Ofc. Cebulski and Ofc. Weaver were inside the building near the victims when the shooter came up the stairs and opened fire, striking Ofc. Cebulski. Weaver returned fire and grazed the shooter in the butt, knocking him down a flight of stairs. This shot wasn't enough to incapacitate him, so the shooter took cover in a vestibule and waited in an ambush position for more officers to come. The guy continued to pop off shots, and the officers finally pinpointed his location. I heard Ofc. Rey Rivera yell, "DOOR 14—HE'S SHOOTING OUT OF DOOR 14." The officers began to move toward the door, and that's when Ofc. Rivera was shot. Then Ofc. Zegar. Then Ofc. Miller.

I realize that I just described the worst day of my life like a police report, yet I haven't been able to do it any other way. I'm sure it's because my life's work has trained me to communicate the indescribable things I've seen in a sequence of sentences. My police mind works by telling stories in chronological order and focusing only on the facts as we know them. No emotion and no speculation. Just cold, hard facts.

But my cops were getting shot. Members of the community I had grown up in were getting shot. One after another. And hearing their voices on the radio after they said they were hit was indescribable. My worst fear as chief was unfolding before me. I felt like I was in the middle of a slow-motion scene in a movie, and all I can remember thinking was "Please make this stop!" I couldn't bear to keep hearing them get shot. Instead, I had to consciously connect to the part of my brain I revert to in a crisis. What needs to be done? Who needs to know? What are the next steps? What is my role? I immediately turned off my emotion like a switch and went into cop mode. I remember thinking that I had to let the mayor know, and when I picked up my phone, the first name I saw in my contacts was Alex Alexandrou, the mayor's chief of staff. I managed to get through to Alex to notify him and the mayor. By that time, we made it to the scene and had to fight the urge to pull right up to the building and join the gunfight as we were instinctively trained to do. As command, our job is to manage the scene—not join the fight.

Because it was an active shooting scene, ambulances couldn't get close enough to gather the wounded officers, so our injured were thrown into squad cars to be transported to the hospital. That meant we didn't have a status on their injuries while we were in the command post communicating with the incident commander, who had taken charge of the perimeter. In serious events, an inner perimeter surrounds the incident taking place. The outer perimeter defines where we set up operations to manage the scene. I didn't know if my officers were dead or alive. I had to keep telling myself to focus on the action happening and deploying the teams inside the building to stop the shooter from killing more people. I kept thinking of the injured officers' families because I knew them all. Then, I received a text message from my wife that simply read, "I'm going in." The shooter was still on the loose, and Ofc. Chris Tunney was with one of the Rescue Task Force teams that deployed for a grid search. Both my ex-husband and my wife work for my department, but more on that later. I read her text, stopped what I was doing for a moment to comprehend the magnitude of what could happen, and responded, "Go find that motherfucker."

Forcing myself to focus on the mission at hand was the hardest thing I've ever had to do. I had several surreal moments when I looked out of the command post and saw a sea of first responders. Nearly all of our Aurora Police Department officers showed up, even those who weren't working. I saw cops in sweatpants running with their rifles toward the perimeter, and cops from every neighboring jurisdiction and beyond were there to assist. We were keeping track of the resources on a whiteboard in the command post, and even though it was all a blur, I recall cops checking in and saying, "Put us wherever you need us." That would be a constant theme from fire, EMS, and police.

This is what I have always loved about first responders. They run toward things that others run away from. Bad cops doing horrible things paint all of us with a broad brush, but every single one on the scene was willing to do whatever was necessary to stop the shooter from killing that day. They put their own lives at risk to save others. The officers who were shot were running into the building to confront the man who was barbarically stealing innocent lives. After Ofc. Gomez was shot, the others pressed on. One by one, they continued to take bullets, but they did not retreat. That is the mindset that cops have, and I will defend noble and honorable police officers until my dying day.

Ninety minutes elapsed as SWAT teams and Rescue Task Force teams went into the three-hundred-thousand-square foot warehouse to search methodically for the active shooter and look for other potential shooting victims. The teams were deploying "nine-bangs" during their search, which are exactly what you would think they are. They emit the sound of gunfire going off (nine times in a row to be exact) and the intent is to make the bad guy believe he's being fired upon. We believe that tactic pushed the shooter further back into the warehouse because the SWAT team made contact with him in a rear corner of the building. The shooter was watching the SWAT operators approach in a perfectly positioned mirror, and when one of our SWAT officers noticed the mirror, he strategically fired some bullets into it, assuming it would shatter, only to learn it was a plastic mirror. The shooter opened fire on the team, but several members diverted, climbed up scaffolding, took a position above the shooter, and shot him before he could hurt any more of our officers. When I heard over the radio that the threat was neutralized, I damn near fell to my knees. Those of us in the command post let out a collective sigh of relief. The shooter was dead, but all that meant was that the action had ceased.

What followed were the worst days of my life. The media was everywhere. There were helicopters in the air, and I was being swooped away to give a press conference. I was told the governor was on his way, and I needed to prepare my remarks. Our public information officer (PIO) had just retired the week before, so Sgt. Bill Rowley was made the interim PIO until we could get a full-time replacement hired. Bill stepped up and managed national and local media as though he had been doing it for years.

By this time, we had a better sense of what occurred from witness accounts. The shooter was called into a termination meeting that afternoon. Among the four people in the meeting with the shooter was Trevor Wehner, a twenty-one-year-old student from Northern Illinois University set to graduate with a degree in human resources in May, and it was his first day working as an intern at the warehouse. After the shooter was told he was being terminated, he stood up, retrieved the .40-caliber handgun from his fanny pack, and shot the management team along with his own union representative as they sat at the conference table. He walked out of the office and chased a man down on a cart and shot him in the back. That guy managed to run out of the warehouse and flag down a passerby in a vehicle who took him to the hospital. We didn't find out about this victim until hours later. According to a witness who was hiding under a desk, the shooter returned to the office and fired more shots at the four victims. He then walked down a set of stairs and shot and killed another employee who worked on the loading dock. The surveillance video followed the shooter as he hunted for more people in the warehouse to kill. That's when officers arrived, and he set his sights on them.

Sgt. Rowley prepared a timeline of the events for me to read at the press conference, but I have never liked reading verbatim from a prepared speech, so I asked for a few moments alone to collect my thoughts for my remarks from the podium. Before everyone scattered from my office, someone pressed a small piece of scrap paper into my hands. When I was alone, I looked down at the paper, which listed the names of the victims. I sat staring at their names.

Josh Pinkard.

Clayton Parks.

Trevor Wehner.

Russell Beyer.

Vicente Juarez.

That Friday, they woke up and went to work. They had no idea that a crazed man getting terminated would shoot them. I held that piece of paper for a long time, and I was paralyzed with grief.

When the governor arrived, I briefed him on the events. He and the mayor spoke, and then I took the podium. At this point, I still had no idea if my officers were all going to pull through, but I knew I had to be strong for them. The national stage was my opportunity to tell *their* story. I know they wished they could have saved the five lives that were taken that day, but they are credited with saving many more. Their response diverted the shooter's attention to them, and they sacrificed their flesh (and potentially their own lives) to stop him from killing. When I read the names of the victims, I tried to do so with such care, knowing that the names crossing my lips were more than "shooting victims." They were human beings with lives and families, and I felt a great sense of responsibility to honor them. That piece of paper with their names scribbled on it sits on my lamp in my office—every day when I turn on the light, I touch the paper and read their names. That paper will go with me into retirement, and it will be with me for the rest of my life as a reminder of the souls who had their lives stolen.

I went to each of their funerals and met their families, and after each one, I got in my squad and sat quietly. I couldn't cry, though. I didn't cry for a long time. I think it was because I felt like I had to keep it together for my people. I couldn't fall apart because I needed to lead us through this, yet I tried to give everyone else permission to feel. But I felt numb.

There was a prayer vigil two days after the shooting, and as I was walked to my squad car when it was over, I saw one of our officers positioned on the perimeter of the large crowd. He was at the scene of the shooting, and here he was suited up and working just forty-eight hours later. The shot officers were placed on leave; so were those who fired rounds from their weapons. But the rest of the officers had to put on their uniforms and get right back to work the same day and the days that followed, even though they went through a traumatic event.

I walked toward the cop. And when you imagine a police officer, this is the guy you visualize. He is ripped, with muscles bulging out of his uniform, and he has full arm sleeves of tattoos. He is your stereotypical badass cop. We locked eyes, and I saw it. I saw the pain, and I felt it in my own body. I went in to give him a hug, but he fell into my arms, sobbing. I absorbed all of him, and I knew at that moment that this was bigger than all of us. He showed me how strong he really was by breaking down. His vulnerability was more courageous than putting on a fake front and saying, "I'm fine." None of us were fine, and he showed me that it was okay not to be okay.

The days that followed were a lot like that. One of the officers in the middle of the shoot-out showed up at my house with his wife, and we drank a bottle of whiskey together. He cried, and I'll never think tears are weak again as long as I live. But I still couldn't cry myself. I felt all the pain, but I couldn't fucking cry.

From this event, I learned that the human spirit is stronger than a coward with a gun. I learned that mindset is everything from Ofc. Adam Miller, who after being shot in the eye, declared over the radio, "I am still in the fight." I watched the citizens of my broken city rise up and collectively put their arms around us. I have never felt more love from my city than during that time, and I am forever grateful to those who made #AuroraStrong the slogan with which we identify. I have watched broken cops slowly heal their bodies and their spirits by acknowledging their pain and pressing on in spite of it. I have seen them cry and fall to their knees only to be lifted by another brother or sister in blue. Above all, I learned that tomorrow is promised to no one and that those who are left with broken hearts but decide to wake up and get through another day are the real heroes.

And then I finally cried. Once I knew our five shot officers were going to live, and once I knew our cops were getting help from professionals, I fell apart when I least expected it. I was in my closet taking off my uniform when I saw I had missed a call from my son, Jacob. I stared at my phone, and as I was about to ring him back, I thought of Trevor, the young intern who was killed. I thought of his mom and how she couldn't call her son ever again. Jacob was nearly the same age as Trevor, and I started to shake. I called Jacob, but he didn't answer. I called him over and over again until he answered:

"Mom, I'm in class—what's wrong?"

My voice cracked. "I needed to hear your voice."

"Of course—I'm walking out of class."

I felt so bad that he had left class that I kept telling him I was sorry. He stayed on the phone with me while I sobbed. I let him go back to class and continued to sob on the floor of my closet. I cried until my head pounded, and I thought of Ofc. Gomez, who only lived because the cops threw him in a squad car and got him to the ER. The doctor told me he was minutes from bleeding out. I thought of Ofc. Cebulski, who took a bullet, and Ofc. Weaver, who applied a tourniquet to him while watching the hallway, ready for the shooter to return. I thought of Ofc. Rivera, Ofc. Zegar, Ofc. Miller, and Sgt. Matt Ziman (my ex-husband), who pinpointed the shooter's location and ran toward the gunfire. I have watched the video of the officers getting shot over and over, and each time I see it, I am reminded of their warrior-like courage. The bullet that went through Ofc. Zegar's neck struck Ofc. Miller in the eye. I have watched the video in slow motion, and it shows Matt yanking his head back milliseconds before a bullet whizzed past his temple. Had he not moved his head, my kids might have lost their dad that day.

These officers are the definition of resilience. Despite a bullet through his neck, Ofc. Zegar had to be physically removed from the scene by Lt. Jeff Wiencek because he wanted to go back in and get the shooter. When I later asked Ofc. Zegar why he fought to leave, he said he thought he was going to die anyway, so why not go back in? That's the mindset of a heroic cop.

CHAPTER TWO

OVERCOMING INK BLOTS

I was born to be a police officer. I wanted to be one of the heroic cops my eventual officers proved themselves to be, like Officer Zegar. I knew at an early age that I wanted to wear a uniform and protect people from bullies. I wanted to run after bad guys and help the good guys because that's what I saw my dad do. My dad was a cop, and I can recall being in our family station wagon when I was about eight years old with him and we saw a horrible crash on the roadway. Although he was off duty, he was never actually off duty because you can't turn off being a police officer when you're with your family. My dad threw the car into park, which jolted me. He told me not to move, and he sprung from the car and ran toward the smoke. I rolled my window down, and the smell of gasoline hit me in the face. I craned my neck and saw my dad dragging people from a car. He laid a woman down on the pavement, and I could see him trying to calm her. He barked out a few orders at some passersby, who slowed down to see what was happening. I think he told them to summon an ambulance since no one had cell phones in the early 1980s.

A few years later, I was riding again with my dad in our family car, and he drew my attention to a car that had just sideswiped a tollbooth. I knew the drill. "Don't move." I stayed in the car and felt like I was in the front row of a movie as my dad ran to the driver's-side door of the car that was still moving slowly past the tollbooth. He opened the car door and put one foot inside the car so he was half running on the street and half inside the moving car. He yanked the gear into park, and then I saw fists flying. This time I got out of the car to get closer because I was older and tougher this time around. I watched as my dad wrestled to get the keys out of the ignition to keep what I later found out was a drunk driver from driving away. I recall the woman working the tollbooth yelling that the police were on the way, and I remember yelling back at her that my dad *is* the police. Sirens roared in the distance, and the officers shook my dad's hand and thanked him for his help and told them they'd take it from there. My dad got back in the car unfazed, and we drove away.

That is why I became a cop. I saw with my own eyes how other cars whizzed by when something was wrong, so I figured out at a young age that first responders run toward things that normal people run away from. If my dad sprang into action off duty wearing Wrangler jeans and cowboy boots, I could only imagine what he did in his uniform at work. At ten years old, my life goal was solidified.

During my high school years, I was known as the future cop. When I attended weekend parties that were starting to get unruly, my best friends were fiercely protective and loyal and would often leave with me before the cops were called. I didn't drink alcohol, but I still knew I could not be in a house with underage drinking or out past curfew. I needed a squeaky-clean record to become a cop. My senior year arrived, and all my friends were applying for colleges and making plans to pack up and move. I, on the other hand, knew I wanted to become a police officer in my hometown. The Aurora Police Department had a "cadet program" that was like an internship. To become a cadet, you had to pass all the same tests required to become a police officer, and if you were lucky enough to get hired, they put you at the top of the list to become a sworn officer upon turning twenty-one. I wanted that job so badly, and I didn't have a plan B. I took the written exam and scored high enough to move onto the next phase of the process that required a psychological exam, a polygraph, background check, and physical agility test.

The polygraph was the first test administered, and I was sweating through my suit. I heard about this test and how your body reacts when telling a lie, so I showed up with the intent to be completely honest. I think it was more than the polygrapher expected because when he asked me if I'd ever stolen anything, I confessed to swiping a chocolate chip cookie that I was explicitly told not to take by my mother while at a picnic. I was ten. When I worked at a sporting goods store at age fifteen, I took a foam stress ball. At sixteen, I lifted face mask clay so I could take it over to my best friend's house because she was grounded. The polygrapher seemed unfazed by my crime spree and also relieved when I stopped confessing. He told me I passed, and I went on to the psychological exam.

I found a journal excerpt from the day I took my psych:

> I passed my polygraph! I will have to wait at least a month before I find out about the psychological. The whole thing was a horrible experience. The testing consisted of five hours of written work (character analysis, common sense, and more character analysis), and the verbal lasted about an hour. The psychiatrist was a stereotypical "mad doctor." He stood about 5'5" and was very round. His hair was salt-and-pepper colored with long wisps from the right side of his head to the left attempting to camouflage his baldness. His bifocals were the most intimidating of all. Every time I answered a question, he peered over them, displaying complete unsatisfaction with my answer. We sat in a little room at a table that was completely glass. He kept looking down at my legs throughout the interview, which made me feel very uncomfortable (I'm guessing that was the point!). He started off by showing me pictures of hands and asked me to tell him what the hands were doing. This was pretty easy for the most part. There were a few gestures that I couldn't come up with anything for right away. Then he showed me ink blots and told me to explain what I saw. I felt like saying that they looked like blots of ink on a piece of paper, but I figured he wouldn't appreciate that! So I just used my imagination and thought

happy thoughts and made up some shit. There was
one, however, that I'm a little nervous about! The
first thought that popped into my head was that it
looked like a dead cat mushed into the pavement.
I wondered if I should say that. I thought it might
show that I have violent tendencies or hate animals
or something terrible. I sat there for a long time and
tried for the life of me to see something other than
the cat, but it was no use. So I told him what I saw.
He looked at me over his bifocals and said, "Really?"
in a disapproving tone. I asked, "Is that bad?" He
ignored me and went on with the rest of the blots.
It seriously looked like a dead cat. Like on Tom and
Jerry cartoons when Tom gets run over by a steam
roller, and he totally looks like a pancake. I can't
wait to find out the results—I'm anxious to know if
I'm sane or not.

Obviously, the dead cat inkblot wasn't a deterrent to my getting hired, but I was worried. These tests to become a police officer
are similar to the ones administered today. This is a question I
often got as the head of my organization. How do we ensure that
"bad apples" don't get into policing? The tests we administer are
good, but not perfect. No test can predict with 100 percent accu-
racy the apple is good. Experts in the field of psychology will tell
you that personality traits emerge in the psychological exam that
can be used to flag those with a propensity for aggression or integrity issues. But these tests are not foolproof because human beings
are complex creatures. The thing that will get you kicked out of the
profession before you get in is lying. The polygraph test is designed

to weed out those who are deceitful. I don't care what you've done that you think you need to cover up—it's a nonstarter. So far, we have not come up with a better system to vet police officers. However, the psychological exam and practitioners have become more advanced. For example, a police agency can tell the psychological examiner what we are seeking in a candidate. When we emphasize traits such as cooperation, problem solving, communication, integrity, etc., the test can be designed in such a way that those who encompass those traits are placed into higher consideration.

These tests serve to weed out the worst apples, but I know that bad apples still manage to fall through the cracks. It is my opinion that the background check is the part of the process where we can determine whether the apple is good. When I was hired, there was no social media, so the background investigator talked to my references, my neighbors, my teachers from high school, and my previous employers. They relied on information from other people to make the determination on whether I was worthy of the profession. Things are very different now, and I think that gives police agencies a great advantage in determining who will become a noble police officer. Unless a person lives off the grid and doesn't use technology (which would be a red flag in and of itself), every one of us moves about the world leaving a digital footprint. If a police applicant is a white supremacist, the likelihood is very high that our background investigators will uncover such activity. Even when someone believes they have scrubbed their digital footprint, something always lingers. Our investigators have bounced candidates for offensive jokes they have posted (or liked) on social media. In some instances, we have given a candidate a chance to explain a questionable post or group to which they belong. Police departments cannot afford to cut corners on background checks of candidates. None of these testing mechanisms are meant to stand alone, but cumulatively, they offer a pretty good assessment of the person who will be receiving a badge. That being said, some rotten apples still find their way in.

I made it through the process, and the first time I put on my cadet uniform, I felt powerful and badass and serious. Very serious. This was a stretch from the person I actually was. I learned quickly that I needed to adapt to my environment and emulate those around me, so I tried to stifle my true personality so as not to draw too much attention to myself. This human survival tactic protects us. But there is a big difference between fitting in and belonging. In *The Gifts of Imperfection*, Brené Brown says, "Fitting in is about assessing a situation and becoming who you need to be to be accepted. Belonging, on the other hand, doesn't require us to change who we are; it requires us to be who we are." I just wanted to fit in, so I lost myself during my years as a cadet. I fell in line with the other cops—we all dressed alike and followed the same barking commands. I could feel myself changing, and I developed a proverbial mask that I dubbed my "cop personality."

I devoted every waking moment to policing. My best friends from high school were all away at college going to parties on the weekend, and I was in a squad car doing back-to-back ride-alongs with cops on Friday and Saturday night. Sometimes a sergeant would tell me to get out of the station and get a life outside of the police department, but I didn't want to do anything but immerse myself in the cop world.

I studied the cops I rode with. I read the giant book of statutes in my free time, and I learned all the elements to crimes. I studied the map books of our city and memorized the hundred blocks so I could get anywhere without looking at the map. That skill has since dissipated because like most of the world, I am a slave to the GPS on my phone. It's been twenty years since I've opened a paper map.

From the moment I started as a cadet, I was counting the days in the calendar until my twenty-first birthday, when I could be a sworn officer. I was like a sponge soaking in police work and learning weird lessons about humanity and its oddities. People don't call 9-1-1 when things are going well, so I got a front-row seat into pain and suffering and death and despair. During these times in the '90s, there was a gang war going on in our city, and we would bounce back and forth to different shooting scenes. I saw more bullet holes in bodies than I could count, and I felt as though I was living in an action movie. But it was real life. The blood shed was real, and the nights on midnight shift in the hospital ER trying to keep distraught family members from storming the operating room was a surreal experience.

In another journal entry during my cadet years, I chronicled the arrest of kid that was brought into our jail for murder. I was assigned to the jail, so it was my responsibility to "book him."

> The trigger man in a gang-related murder was caught today. We had him in booking, and I had to finger-print him and book him into the computer. He was just a kid. He was about sixteen years old, and he had the sweetest disposition. While I was printing him, I realized the hands I was touching pulled the trigger of a deadly weapon and took someone's life. Those hands were as normal as mine. It's his heart that is

different from mine. When I put him in his jail cell, I said to him, "It's a shame you're going to get yourself killed because I was starting to like you." He looked at me with a smirk and asked what I meant. I told him if he keeps with this gang shit, he's going to die. He laughed and said he's always careful. He thinks he's indestructible. I feel sorry that his life is going to turn out badly because there was a chance for him. There's a chance for everyone who is willing.

I didn't include his name in my journal entry or else I'd research to see if my prediction was accurate. I'll never know what became of him after he went through the juvenile court system. I was so idealistic, and I actually believed that I could be the kind of police officer who made a difference. I've become more calloused over the years, but I'm still that same twenty-year-old who wrote the journal entry. I still believe that people are inherently good, and I believe in second chances.

CHAPTER THREE

PIRATE SHIPS AND SLIM JIMS

An eight-year-old walks into a bar.

That's not a punchline.

I was raised in a bar, although it wasn't officially called a bar. It was the Fraternal Order of Eagles, and my family called it "the club." Like many private members-only clubs of its time, the members were all white men. Women were allowed, but they couldn't be full-fledged members—not until many years later, when the clubs were running out of money. But as part of the ladies' auxiliary, women were allowed to organize the potlucks. That's what Mom did.

Every day, after my cop dad got off work at 3:00 p.m., he picked me up from Aurora Christian School and drove us to the club. The shabby building was tucked away down a winding road behind a Long John Silver's restaurant. Inside the vestibule, a camera stared blankly at us as Dad stuck his membership card in a slot. On the other side, a black-and-white monitor behind the bar showed the bartender who was coming and going. He buzzed us in. After the guys at the bar greeted Dad by name, I scurried off to play by myself. I wasn't allowed to sit at the bar, so I found things to occupy my time. In an adjacent hall, where the ladies' auxiliary organized potlucks at long tables, I constructed a clubhouse from the clunky metal chairs with vinyl cushions and hunkered down to read and draw pictures. While I sprawled under the table, a guy named Lenny buffed and polished the floors to a high shine.

When I got bored and whiny, I pestered my dad at the bar:

"Daddy, I'm borrrrred. When are we going home?"

"Soon. Here are some quarters. You want a Slim Jim?"

I knew the routine. The quarters, for arcade games—Q*bert and Centipede—would buy Dad some time at the bar where he slugged down beers. Fortunately, he was a giddy drunk; the more beers he drank, the happier he was. When he was full-on jolly, I got a Tombstone pizza. I could hear it happening because the metal pizza oven behind the bar made a squeaky noise when the bartender pulled the handle to set the pizza inside. Knowing that pizza was for me, I stopped bugging him to leave. We usually headed for home around 6:00 p.m. because that was the time Mom got home from her job as a secretary. Dad was a cop by day but an alcoholic by night. Dependent on Dad, Mom was likely clinically depressed during my teenage years, but I wasn't keen enough to understand such things.

Oddly enough, growing up in a bar had its perks. Aside from the obvious benefits of junk food and arcade games, I learned to communicate with adults at an early age. Because I was rarely with other kids, I talked to adults all the time. Though Dad would chide me for talking their ears off, I found most of the patrons who frequented the establishment were good, working-class people. Naturally, I didn't realize then that they, too, were bellied up to a bar every day because something in their life was broken. Most of them added to my pile of quarters and talked to me like an adult— they were kind to me. As I look back on my twisted life, I realize that my strong communication skills were built in that dingy club.

When the weekend rolled around, Dad was the first one up in the morning. Around 6:00 a.m., I smelled coffee brewing and shuffled out of my room to see him holding the big newspaper in front of him, a cup of coffee and cigarette nearby on the end table. I'd run as fast as I could from the hallway and leap toward him to mess up his newspaper. I never succeeded because he always heard me coming, and with quick reflexes, he moved the newspaper so I couldn't crinkle it when I came in airborne. He made room for me by wrapping his right arm around both my shoulders so I was tucked in tight next to him while he read. Dad already had the comics section of the paper waiting for me, so I could transfer the ink from *Family Circus* to a wad of Silly Putty, Mom's contribution. Dad nicknamed me "Silly Putty" from my obsession with this ritual and called me that until he died in 2016.

I loved watching Dad cook breakfast for me on Sunday mornings. He made the bacon first, set aside with paper towels strewn over the crispy strips to keep them warm, and then he cracked eggs into the bacon grease in the same pan. He never flipped the eggs. Instead, he used the spatula to flick bacon grease on top of the eggs to cook them. I still make over-easy eggs like this on the rare occasion I eat bacon. After breakfast, he got dressed and asked me if I wanted to go to the club with him. My answer always depended on Marcy and Heather, my best friends in the neighborhood. If they were around, I opted to play with them, but when they weren't—which was more often than not—I'd go with Dad. Weekends at the club were different from weeknights; it still smelled of stale beer, but there was a different vibe in the daylight. And Dad allowed me to go outside if I wore him down. On these occasions, he handed me a five-dollar bill, and I set off down the winding road to the Long John Silver's, where I ordered hush puppies, and the lady behind the counter gave me a paper pirate hat. It was reserved for the kids' fish-and-chips meal, but she always broke the rules and gave me a hat. With my pirate hat on, I pretended the kitschy patio was my ship and I the captain, forcing imaginary crew and hostages to walk the plank and poking them with my imaginary sword. Hours rolled by on my fake ship, but I would eventually find my way back to the club, where I had to ring the doorbell to get the bartender's attention to be let back in.

This was my childhood from seven until my teens. As an only child, I had to entertain myself, and from my narrow perspective, I felt lucky I had a pirate ship and a shiny-floored hall to play in at the club. I had friends at my private Christian school, but rarely did I see them outside of school. They all lived in mansions (in my mind) while my house was the size of a Cracker Jack box. Even at the age of eight, I knew I didn't want my friends to come over. Plus, Dad could be unpredictable. Despite being a jovial man at the bar, he had a dark side that only Mom could bring out. She yelled at him for spending so much time at the club, which put him in a bad mood and seemed to make him drink more. My mom was right to

chide him for drinking, but I hated the predictable cycle of his reaction. He was never abusive to us, but he often brought down his
fist on the table or his ashtray, rattling my teeth and the windows.
I begged Mom to leave him alone, so he wouldn't be mad. But she
kept at him, he kept drinking, and I kept finding him passed out on
the only toilet we had in the house. I lost track of the times I woke
up having to pee only to find him there. I had no other choice but
to squeeze past him and relieve myself, my little butt hanging over
the edge of the bathtub. To me, this was normal—normal because
you don't know what you don't know as a child.

The years went on, and I grew into a chubby preteen from all
the Tombstone pizzas and Slim Jims. When I outgrew the pirate
hat, I started playing billiards at the club. I was allowed to rack
the balls only when the men weren't playing, and I spent hours
perfecting my shots. Every week, an old drunk guy would stag-
ger over and make a bet with me, believing I was just a kid with
no skills. I always took his bet and then cleaned the table. I made
more money winning bets playing pool than I collected in allow-
ance. I saved up and bought myself a pool cue with its very own
carrying case. But I didn't let anyone see me retrieve it from the
case until after they called my bet.

Eventually, I was old enough to stay home alone, so I stopped
going with Dad to the club. Mom and Dad's marriage crumbled,
largely due to his drinking and infidelity with a handful of dis-
patchers at the police department. Dad moved out when I was
fourteen, but for two years, my parents tried to reconcile numer-
ous times, and each time, we would be waiting for him. On one
occasion, my mom and I made signs that said, "Welcome Home!"
I didn't understand how pathetic it was to welcome him back from

the latest tryst; I was happy to have him home because it meant he would cut back on his drinking, which meant my parents would broker a temporary ceasefire.

This cycle of moving out and moving back in continued until I was sixteen. By then, I was over it. Every time Dad left, Mom would close the curtains and lie on the sofa. Throughout my formative years, she was a woman who gardened, taught fitness classes at the Y, made candles from scratch, and painted ceramics. She stopped doing all the things she loved, and it was heartbreaking to watch. When this happened, I tried to take care of her, but then I got tired of convincing her to get up. I started going home with my best friends Carrie and Beth after school, where their parents would feed me and allow me to sleep over without asking questions. Eventually, I stopped going home. I pretended I was Carrie's fifth sibling. The Fisher family (yes, her name is Carrie Fisher) never made me feel like an outsider, and her parents made me do my homework with all the other kids. For the first time in my life, I didn't feel part of something dysfunctional. To this day, I believe the Fishers saved me from what I might have become. In confronting the realities of my upbringing, I see how my life could have turned out very differently.

It's ironic how the skills I learned from being forced into a dysfunctional childhood manifested positively in my adulthood. The paradox of my dad was that he battled the demons of substance abuse—Mom said alcohol was always his first mistress—but he never verbally or physically abused us. I never doubted for a moment how much he loved me and how proud he was of me. I constantly heard him brag about me to the other club patrons, telling them not to mess with me because I was a tough chick and a pool shark to boot. I developed into a creative, imaginative person because Mom constantly bought me markers, pens, and art kits—all the things I wanted. I realize now that it was to preoccupy me at the club. I became an independent, resilient, confident woman who finally stopped eating Slim Jims. I went on to follow in my father's footsteps as a police officer, took the good things my parents gave me, and opted to use the rest as a lesson in what not to do in my life. I learned not to drink alcohol to excess. I learned to be a better parent. I learned not to be submissive to an unfaithful person. I vowed never to wallow in despair on the sofa for anyone. I learned to be independent and unafraid because I was completely unsupervised most of the time. I learned to be the captain of my own ship, and I got comfortable making people walk the plank.

These are the same lessons I would learn about leadership in my career—what not to do. I was the chief of the police department in the second-largest city in Illinois. I'm a cop. I carry a gun. Shouldn't that be leadership enough? Not when you consider that every other member of my organization also carries a gun. Unless I want a staff meeting to devolve into a modern showdown at the O.K. Corral, I need to be a leader, not just the boss, and not just the person with the biggest gun or the fastest draw. I didn't understand until recently how my colorful childhood prepared me to be a cop and how my experiences molded me into becoming the first female police chief in the second-largest police department in Illinois. We are all manifestations of our life experiences, and it's easy to blame our hardships for our lot in life or our failures. Every obstacle thrown your way serves to build resilience and grit. And each obstacle can be used as a stepping stone to move onward and upward.

Growing up in a bar couldn't prepare me for the challenges in policing that I would incur over my career. The resilience I'd built in my childhood on my fake pirate ship wasn't enough to help me navigate the impending storms of a mass shooting, a pandemic, and civil unrest that loomed.

CHAPTER FOUR

PERFECT STORM

On the now-infamous video, I heard George Floyd tell Ofc. Chauvin that he couldn't breathe sixteen times. A bystander was telling Floyd to get up and get in the car, and Floyd continued to say, "I can't." Chauvin never took his knee off of Floyd's neck even after he went unconscious. Floyd wasn't actively resisting, and bystanders were screaming that Floyd was not moving. Chauvin still kept his knee firmly on Floyd's neck until he took his last breath.

I remember watching the footage and asking myself, "What in the actual fuck?" Nothing that I saw warranted the actions taken by the officers that day. I'm still unclear why they removed Floyd from the squad car in the first place. Nothing in the police training manual allows for this excessive use of a restraint. The only time an officer may use deadly force in such a manner is if that officer or another is at risk of being seriously harmed or killed. None of that was happening. Floyd died under the knee of a cop. Nay, Derek Chauvin murdered a man in broad daylight giving zero care or concern for his welfare.

After watching the video, I took action. I was bold and courageous. I risked my career and my own safety by sending a tweet: "Resisting suffocation is not resisting arrest. People of color are outraged. White people are outraged. Any cop who doesn't feel the same should get out of our profession."

See? I am "woke." I sat courageously behind my computer screen and tweeted those words to show that a line had been crossed. Look at how progressive I am!

I hope you were reading that in the sarcastic tone for which it was intended because there is nothing courageous about tweeting the obvious. There was no risk to me in pointing out the heinous action of a rogue cop. Those who possess even a minuscule amount of intellect cannot find any justification for kneeling on a man's neck. I did find it puzzling that it took time for some cops to come to that conclusion. I heard them say, "We don't have all the facts" or "I'll refrain from judgment until I know the full story." I don't care if George Floyd had stuck a fork in the eye of the convenience-store clerk when he was buying cigarettes with a counterfeit bill. I don't care if George Floyd was high on *all* the drugs. He was not resisting. He was handcuffed and lying chest down on the pavement with a knee obstructing his airway for over nine minutes. There is nothing that could have justified Chauvin's actions, and I didn't need to wait for more facts.

But that's exactly the angle the defense offered in the Chauvin trial. Floyd did have drugs in his system. Floyd was not a model citizen. He had a sordid history; therefore, the actions must have been justified. Of further absurdity was to claim that Chauvin's knee wasn't actually on his neck and possibly on his back. I watched him die after declaring he couldn't breathe, so I call that a "clue" in my profession.

Groupthink finally allowed the lagging cops to agree it was wrong. The lack of courage in our profession to denounce the actions of a fellow brother in blue was disheartening. But as soon as the majority called it out, the rest were safe to do so. Most noble police officers know when a cop has messed up, but not everyone speaks up. So when they do, it is courage on display. When the verdict for Chicago police officer Jason Van Dyke was being announced for the shooting of Laquan McDonald, I saw a bunch of cops standing around the television in the common area of our police department waiting to hear his fate. When the guilty verdict was announced, a cop bellowed, "Oh great—now we can't even do our jobs anymore!" I was on the staircase landing above them, and I was stunned at the cop's reaction. Fortunately, I didn't have to say a word because one of the courageous officers standing in the group retorted, "No—we just can't shoot someone walking away from us in the back sixteen times." The rest of the cops all agreed in the affirmative. But that one who felt that he couldn't do his job anymore, he and others like him are the problem at its core.

One of the greatest flaws in my profession is the inability to objectively assess the actions of a fellow cop. The good cops are critical and call balls and strikes, but so many say they don't want to "armchair quarterback" another cop's decision-making. That analogy has always been curious to me considering that professional sports teams literally dissect game footage frame by frame to determine exactly where they went wrong and how they can make the play better. If every cop did the same for each use-of-force incident, we would improve as a profession. Due process is one thing, but blind loyalty is something else. Until that changes, nothing in policing will change. Until unions are stripped of the power to get a bad cop's job back, nothing will change. Unions are crucial to ensuring that cops get compensated and working conditions are equitable, and I have been fortunate to have a great union fighting for my benefits, but unions should not have as much power as they do in the disciplinary process. The rebuttal is that it's crucial to protect cops from rogue members of management. I've worked for rogue supervisors, and I understand that power can be abused, so let's find a new alternative. Let's have a judicial review by a magistrate who rules by case law and consistency and not arbitrators whose bread and butter is to get hired to hear the case. Fix that, and you will have actually done something to reform policing.

If you're a cop, you've probably stopped reading or you are seething right now. If you are feeling angry at my words, I invite you to explore why. We all say cliché things like "No one despises a bad cop more than a good cop," yet some in blue don't walk that talk.

The riots that unfolded days after the murder of Floyd were a result of a match thrown into flammable gas that has been lingering in the air. As a nation, we were divided by politics, and our president was doing little to unite us. What resulted was a division like I've never experienced in my lifetime. We are all used to partisan politics, but at the end of the day, there has been a mutual respect despite policy differences. We have always seemed to navigate around partisanship, and even when things got heated, we were still united as a people. Regardless of your politics, most agree that Trump wasn't a unifier of *all* people. But to say he isn't a leader would be inaccurate because I have never seen the likes of followership as I have seen in his base. Suffice it to say, the dividing line between Never Trumpers and MAGA was definitive, and you couldn't straddle the middle. Friendships dissolved and family dinners were strained and uncomfortable when politics collided. Online dating profiles made clear distinctions not to swipe if politics didn't align. Trump supporters were dubbed racist. Anyone on the other side was dubbed an anti-police "snowflake." Everywhere we turned, there was friction.

Then a pandemic struck, and we all got really scared, and I thought that might be the thing that would bring us together. It was a virus, and one cannot refute the science behind an infectious disease, right? Nope, only we Americans could succeed in making COVID a partisan issue. I am still astounded by the train wreck we all were (are). We associated mask wearing with the Democrats and denying that the coronavirus was even a real thing with the Republicans. And those of us in the middle (henceforth referred to as the reasonable ones who had not lost their minds) were scratching our heads at this alternate universe in which we found ourselves living.

As we were hoarding toilet paper and washing the packaging of our groceries wearing our hazmat suits, a cop killed a black man in Minneapolis, Minnesota, and that was the proverbial straw. Law enforcement was already suffering from trust erosion as more and more people began to capture footage of police brutality. Politics were heated and our nation divided, and we were getting sick and losing loved ones from COVID. People were out of work and financially strapped. Tensions were high in our homes because we were all cooped up together. And the sparks turned into flames. A nation at the end of its rope resulted in a fury of chaos. And our cities burned.

Violence erupted, crime skyrocketed, and the world remained divided. This time it felt as though it was everyone united against the police. This was our new civil rights movement, and we still have not recovered from it. Despite my strong feelings about the actions of Chauvin, I have the intellectual capacity to understand that he does not represent who we are as a profession. The majority of cops show up to work and do their jobs with professionalism and compassion. I wanted to proclaim to my city and the rest of the nation we all did not kill George Floyd, and it was unfair to be treated as though we had. But conceptually, I understand that we are all painted with a broad brush. As much as I could feel something without experiencing it personally, I understood the pain that our ancestors inflicted and how even in our progression toward equality, we aren't even close to where we should be.

Floyd's murder on May 25, 2020, was the day that flipped the switch in the police world. This incident started a trajectory in my own career that has caused me to question everything I believe about policing. The day I felt a sense of unity and relief was the day Chauvin was convicted of murder. Some cops stopped short of believing he should go to jail. They capitulated to the fact he shouldn't have kneeled on his neck, but to put a cop in jail for doing his job was a stretch for some. I got tired of hearing some cops jump on the "George Floyd is not a hero" bandwagon. He's not. But he did not deserve to die.

CHAPTER FIVE

ILLUSION OF POWERLESSNESS

Almost all the headlines and articles about the George Floyd murder made mention of "power." The discourse surrounding Floyd's murder focused on the power gap between Floyd and Chauvin. The term "power" gets slung around in many different arenas. I hear it commonly used to describe control of others in a negative way. We often hear of the term "abuse of power" and its correlation to the police or other government officials. Al Gini describes power as possessing the capacity to control or direct change. That description doesn't label power as negative, and it's true that all forms of leadership make use of power. Leadership is about creating meaning in people's lives, and it can be toxic and fear based or moral and just. This is the dynamic of power, and Gini rightfully asks, "Will it be used wisely and well?" Therein lies the struggle. To say that someone possesses the capacity to control or direct acknowledges that he is in a position of power over another. One doesn't have to have a formal title to be in a position of authority to influence, but it's arguably difficult to abuse power without holding a position of leadership or authority.

I have watched the powerful very carefully, and the way people act in each lot in life is telling of their character. How a person wields his or her power is so revealing. Power feels good. It feels good to have a command presence where people actually listen and comply. I'm only a police chief of a midsized organization, but I understand that the title of chief affords me power. The operative word in that sentence is "title" because it isn't referring to the individual. It's the position I hold. When I was first appointed, it was strange to hear people calling me "chief." Now, I rarely hear my actual name anymore. I have formal authority by rank, but I also had power before I attained any rank. I thought of myself as powerless as a rank-and-file officer because I fell at the bottom of the hierarchy structure, but I realize now that wasn't true. My badge gave me power over others. I understand that my believing I had no power was an illusion.

I can see how some people become hypnotized by power. When I ask someone to do something, they do it. It's magical and empowering. When I attend events, I get introduced and have to stand up and wave. I even found that I receive preferential treatment at restaurants and businesses. To say the chief patronizes an establishment carries clout, so people capitalize on it. Here's the rub. It has nothing to do with me. All the perceived power is attached by others to the position. I am enlightened to this concept, so it's easy for me not to believe that there is something special or unique about me. Many people in positions of power get sucked into the flattery and elitism, and they begin to believe they are better than everyone else. They get addicted to people kissing their asses. I view over-the-top compliments and flattery the same way I view insults and bullying. I discard both. I don't think it's healthy for a person to believe what people say on either end of the spectrum. Even in this example, it is more about a position than anything else.

I worked for a commander who loved power. I had this recurring cartoon image in my imagination of him sitting over a chessboard where the pawns were people in our department. He'd pick us up by the skin of the back of our necks like little puppies and move us all around and knock us off the board, so he and his cronies would have the advantage. The image of us all kicking and squirming as he picked us up and moved us around offered some comical imagery for me until I realized the dynamic was real. He was extremely calculated and very charming, so when you got knocked off, it left you feeling bewildered.

The powerful often feel as though rules don't apply to them, and the commander displayed examples of the "Do as I say, not as I do" phenomenon. He made a big deal about officers' letting their cars warm up. We had a policy about idling cars, and it was his pet peeve when he saw empty squads warming up in the lot of the department. He would bellow about it and call someone to make sure that officer knew he noticed. This is one of those policies that makes no sense. In the Chicago area, especially in winter, anyone who has a rational thought understands that the car has to warm up. To depart with a cold engine is not only bad for the car but really uncomfortable for the officer.

One day, I was walking by my administrative assistant's desk, and she asked if I'd seen the commander. I told her I had not. She replied, "Okay, if you see him, let him know the city garage called, and his automatic car starter is done being installed on his squad."

I stopped walking and looked at her. "What did you say?" She repeated the exact same sentence. I think I said what I was thinking out loud. "Are you kidding me?" Commanders had take-home squad cars, and despite his coming down on the officers who simply wanted to get into a warm car at the beginning of their shift when it was twenty below zero, this joker had an automatic starter installed so he could warm (or cool) his car? The hypocrisy was so thick that I actually started laughing. It was perceived power that afforded him the luxury of the rule bent in his favor. In this case, the rule was more snapped in half than bent, but you get the idea.

There are people who thrive on power, and he was one of them. He harmed our organization because he had power over others, and he could skip over people or knock people down because he was running the board. Even the chief at the time did nothing to rein him in. When I was in his crosshairs, I felt ter-rorized and helpless because he had power over my career. This is a great sob story, right? I have used words like "terrorized" and "harmed" to describe some bad bosses I've had to endure. Yes, they affected my career and caused a great deal of stress in my life, but the truth is, I don't know the first thing about being harmed. I was a police officer with a great salary and great bene-fits, and I went home at the end of my workday and complained to my spouse about the commander. We concocted hypotheses about his childhood that might explain his Machiavellian tenden-cies and concluded that his mom and dad didn't tell him they were proud of him enough. We laughed about it and then went to sleep in our warm bed in our big suburban house.

I'm embarrassed to say that my vantage point of power has been limited to my own narrow scope. I can spout off abuses of power from bad bosses, but I largely thought of these abuses as individually driven. By that I mean it was the person in power doing a bad thing to keep people down in the organization. I convinced myself that the "man" was trying to keep me down! As a woman in a male-dominated profession, I have been a victim of the system, fought the man, and won! I am sitting in the big chair to prove it. I have lived my leadership life combating abuse of power. I have tried to give away as much power as I could at the police department by relinquishing control of systems that were in place. I took the power away from the position of chief for the promotional process. Before, the chief could slash or lower an officer's rating by ten points in either direction with no explanation. I hated the cloak of secrecy that went along with that, so I got rid of it and pushed the power to middle management, who has a better grasp of performance. I have patted myself on the back for giving power away, and I convinced myself that I was a righteous leader in doing so. But I was delusional because the truth is, I have never experienced true powerlessness. Abuse of power is about using authority to unjustly inflict harm upon another, and I was certain that I was harmed by that definition. But it's relative. I grew up as a white woman who *chose* to enter a male-dominated profession. I have worn a uniform since I was twenty-one years old, so I have wielded power over others for all of my adult life. Yeah, a few tormentors gave me a hard time, but this was hardly oppression. And I see now that slewing around a phrase like "abuse of power" to describe hardships at work is irresponsible of me now that my eyes are finally opened. I have failed to see (failed to look) beyond my own narrow scope to actual abuses of power. I didn't understand the depth and breadth of power until I started seeking the vantage point of those who have experienced true powerlessness. Only now am I beginning to attempt to understand what I didn't before.

SANDRA BLAND

The officer's actions in the Floyd case are indefensible, but it's not usually that clear. There are many high-profile cases that aren't as definitive. When the story of Sandra Bland's suicide in jail hit the headlines, I remember wanting to know more. Suicides are not out of the ordinary, and as a police officer, I've responded to many of them. They are always heartbreaking to witness, but so are all scenes where someone has died. I heard the same details about Sandra Bland that everyone else did when it flashed on the evening news, and that's what made it more puzzling to me. She was pulled over for a traffic violation, and the officer arrested her for obstruction because she refused to get out of the car. She went to jail and took her own life in her cell. I remember thinking that it seemed like a disproportionate response to a simple obstruction charge, and my fleeting thought was that she must have had some underlying depression or mental health issues for her to have committed suicide. That incident happened in Texas but made the Chicago news because she lived in the Midwest before heading south. I recall thinking it was tragic and horrifying that her story ended that way and wondered what exactly drove her to take her own life—if that's really what happened.

Then, I read Malcolm Gladwell's book, *Talking to Strangers*.

I am a Gladwell junkie, and I have read every book he's written, subscribed to his podcasts, and made it my hobby to hang on his every word. In the beginning of the book, Gladwell leads with Sandra Bland's story and recounts the real-time dialogue between Trooper Brian Encinia and Ms. Bland during the traffic stop. By this time, I'd heard the dialogue from the squad camera footage on the news, so I knew how it transpired. In my assessment, the cop had been polite and communicative, and from what I deducted, she was rude to him. She snapped at him and then lit up a cigarette in her car. He told her to put it out, but she didn't. All she had to do was get out of the car, but she refused to do that, too.

But as the sentences in the book continued to build, I got the feeling that Gladwell was about to bash the cop and suggest he did something wrong. I stopped reading, panicked, and held an inner dialogue with Malcolm (we are on a first-name basis in my head): "Malcolm, don't ruin my love for you. Don't make me put this book down and break up with you. We have a good thing going where you write words, and I read them, and I get smarter and fall deeper in love with you."

Despite Gladwell's already having sold millions of copies of his books, I was certain he would know if I stopped buying them. I stared at the book for a moment and made the decision to press on.

You should have already deduced that I am not one of those cops who automatically sides with other cops. But Sandra Bland's incident was different. She didn't comply. The cop didn't kill her. She killed herself. These incidents are not even in the same stratosphere.

I reluctantly picked up the book and continued reading, and I'm not afraid to admit that my discomfort mounted with every single word I read. Gladwell brilliantly dissected the encounter from the vantage point of both the police officer and Sandra Bland. And as I read, Gladwell transported me to a place that Oprah would call an "ah-ha" moment. For the first time in my life, I was able to transcend into the world view of Sandra Bland. Do not misinterpret my words. I will never know what it is like to move about the world as a person of color. I have lived in my white skin all my life and will never know anything else, but for the first time in my life, I felt the anger that Sandra Bland must have felt when she moved over to the side of the road so the officer could go around her, only to discover that she was being pulled over for failing to signal. That's why she was snippy with him at the onset. What the cop didn't know was that her life had been a tapestry of red tape from other similar violations that caused her a great deal of financial burden. She wasn't a violent offender. And in this case, she was instinctively moving out of the cop's way, believing he wanted to get around her.

But the cigarette. That's where she really went wrong. She lit up a cigarette while the cop was standing at her window. Did she light that cigarette as an act of defiance? Or did she just really need a cigarette in that moment of nervousness? Whatever the reason, it broke bad when she refused to put it out. It's not illegal to light a cigarette in your own vehicle. It's not even illegal to refuse to put it out if a cop requests that you do so. But it is illegal to refuse to exit the vehicle when requested by a cop. And that's why she was arrested.

Cops see simply that she refused to get out of the car. Why is compliance so difficult? How dare she not put out the cigarette when asked? And she was rude from the onset of the encounter, and the cop was polite. I have heard myself say that failing to comply is the common denominator to all the bad things happening, and I'm still not ready to relinquish that position. Even if I agree that the cop who pulled over Sandra Bland made a weak traffic stop, that is enough for some to justify failing to comply, but for me it's not. Even if you believe you are being wronged, it is more dangerous to resist or obstruct than it is to comply. That sentence alone is the very essence of the dissenting argument— police have too much power.

And I also concede the fact that I'd think differently if this was the fiftieth time I'd been stopped by the police for minor violations. Isn't that what causes the anger that turns to resisting? Probably. And yes, I agree that the root of the problem is the number of times these individuals were stopped or the minor reasons they were stopped (a disparity when you compare white people pulled over). I hear all of this. But I can't get to a place of accepting that a person should defy and resist. I believe it's putting the noncompliant person at greater risk.

The person who has come closest to swaying me is author Dr. Ibram X. Kendi. I heard him talking on Oprah's Super-Soul Sunday to a group of people about Sandra Bland. He said, "Why was it her job to de-escalate the encounter with the cop?" I froze for a moment and analyzed his question. Ms. Bland was pissed about getting pulled over. She was minding her own business trying to get to her destination to start her new life, and she was tired. She was tired of driving and tired of getting pulled over, so when it happened again for something so minor, she wasn't kind to the officer. She was outwardly rude and argumentative, and that caused the officer to mirror her demeanor. But why? Why did he have to succumb to it? Her rudeness toward him is what I believe made him snap about the cigarette. Dr. Kendi questioned why it was her responsibility to de-escalate and not the officer's, and I think that brilliant question has caused a shift in my paradigm. It was ego. He got mad because she was mad. She questioned his authority. Did that have to happen? That is the entire premise of Gladwell's book. I realized that Dr. Kendi was asking the same question that Gladwell had asked but in a different way. Had the cop not gotten offended that Ms. Bland was challenging his power and authority, might the encounter have ended differently?

I was discussing this incident with my mentor and friend, Dr. Vincent Gaddis. He is a professor and subject matter expert on issues of race, class, and social justice, and he is an African American man. He listened to my rant and got frustrated with me:

"You didn't mention race at all!"

"Wait? How do you even know race played a factor? The cop didn't say anything to give that impression. It's all recorded."

"Do you really honestly believe that if Sandra Bland were white, she would be dead?"

Dr. Gaddis believed the cop's bias or racism was the power that supplemented his aggressive action. He told me it was disingenuous to discuss this incident without bringing up race, but I didn't bring it up because I can't know for sure what was inside the cop's head.

POLICE DISCRETION

Let's unpack this. Yes, there was likely a violation of the law, and it is our job as law enforcement to tend to these matters. However, I am willing to admit that some outcomes are based on demeanor.

When I pull someone over, I have the discretion to determine the level of enforcement I assign to the violator. If that violator is respectful and polite, I might not write him or her a ticket if the infraction was minor. However, if that violator gets snippy with me, my pen is going to be put to use. That is the essence of power and exactly what Dr. Kendi was trying to make us see.

Of course, some cops adhere consistently to the law and write as many tickets to kind grandmas and soccer moms as they do to those who mouth off to them. Yes, there are cops who don't care who is behind the wheel, but I am going to push back ever so gently (hard) to say that discretion is in the eye of the enforcer. Applying discretion to serve yourself is a form of manipulation, so the only adaptation made in any situation should be with the best outcome in mind. If someone has violated the law, it is the responsibility of the officer to determine what action will ensure that the violator doesn't do it again. Sometimes a warning will suffice while other times people don't change their behavior until they have to pay a fine. But if a cop isn't thinking in terms of best outcomes, the method they choose to enforce the law will be inconsistent.

I started to reflect and it finally became crystal clear to me. If bias or prejudice of any form were allowed to creep in, might it be in the gray area of discretion? Even if you are not racist, might you see where *possessing power over another* could cause issues for a cop who is? Discretion is the space where cops can exercise their power based on their bias against gender, class, or race, and it will be supported by the institution. That is the loophole. And as a cop who has admittedly been influenced by people who weren't respectful (this is a nice way of saying I will write you a ticket if you give me a hard time), I think it's time we illuminate the dark corners of policing and open our eyes to the consequences of this disproportion.

Power.

This is the imbalance of power that I am now beginning to understand. But first let's talk about the necessity of law enforcement because I'm *not* turning on my profession. I believe that in a democracy, there must be people charged with keeping peace and order. In Plato's *The Republic*, Socrates outlined a utopian society to include the "guardians." He said that democracy must have guardians present to ensure the safety of our citizens and do what is best for the city. *The Republic* was written in 375 BC, well before the modern police officer existed, but Socrates seemed to understand that guardianship must be carried out by those who care about a community and the people in it.

We are a nation of laws. That is not to say that some laws are not antiquated and riddled in racism, classism, sexism, and all the "isms." When I offered this to Dr. Gaddis, he schooled me again:

"Let me go Kendi on you. Laws or policies are racist or anti-racist, so we cannot just say we are a nation of laws; we are a nation of racist laws, sexist laws, and policies. These laws and policies perpetuate the very biases you seek to change."

This is why Dr. Gaddis is one of my most trusted advisors. He assertively forces me to see (look) where I wouldn't if I were left to my own devices. We often meet for breakfast, and he can polish off a plate of bacon and simultaneously compel me to confront my blind self. The crux of the issue that Dr. Gaddis brought up about the laws themselves being racist, classist, or sexist is precisely what requires a shift in thinking. It's about inequity in policing. The "war on drugs" is a great illustration of this. All the white people who got busted with cocaine were not punished as severely as the black people who possessed crack because laws were passed to make sure of that. It's the same infraction from an illegal possession of a controlled substance standpoint, but white people got a slap on the wrist while our jails began filling up disproportionately with black people because the punishment was far harsher. Cocaine conjures up images of white guys wearing button-down shirts with the sleeves rolled up cutting white power with a razor blade on a mirror. But crack is different, right? It must be since black people were targeted, searched, arrested, and convicted for the same thing, and many black lives have been ruined because of the disparity. The white guys with cocaine charges are doing just fine. If this example alone doesn't convince you that the system of laws were disproportionate, I don't know what will. The war on drugs was a war on black people. Period.

I doubt this is what Socrates had in mind when he referred to police as the "guardians" of democracy. The demand for criminal justice reform isn't new to us. George Floyd's death may have been the bubbling-over point, but through the years, law enforcement executives and scholars have attempted to fix what was broken. In fact, Socrates is probably laughing in the afterlife with all of his philosopher friends at the present-day phrases we've come up with to describe what he already knew in 375 BC: "procedural justice," "fair and impartial policing," and "police legitimacy" are word salads to say that police officers need to treat people fairly and apply the law consistently so the community they police trusts them. Holy crap, we sure overcomplicate things for the sake of catchphrases and buzzwords, but those words are empty if our actions aren't aligned.

All of this to say that we have failed as guardians if we are (or are perceived as) abusing power. If black and brown people don't feel protected by the police, we are failing. If members of our community feel terrorized by the police, we are failing. My cop tribe needs to listen (hear) the battle cries from the voices who speak for Sandra Bland and others like her and try to understand how we have failed.

Before the death of George Floyd, I thought I understood power, and I genuinely thought I was oppressed by my tormentors: a bad boss, for example. I was so proud of navigating the waters filled with sharks who were out for blood. I convinced myself that I fought the "man" and won and that if I could penetrate the glass ceiling in policing, anyone could accomplish anything. I was so blinded by my own perception of powerlessness in privilege that I couldn't see real and true powerlessness. Even though my police department and my officers didn't kill George Floyd, we represent the disparity of power in policing, and it's about time we open our eyes to the realities of racism by admitting it exists. That is the root of the power dynamic in this country. Many believe that is the root of what went wrong with Sandra Bland and George Floyd. Others believe race had nothing to do with either incident. None of us were inside the head of Chauvin, so we don't know why he put his knee on a man's neck, causing him to die. Chauvin didn't make a racial slur in the process of killing George Floyd, but I could see clearly that he didn't value his life or his humanity. Why not? If a white man was beneath his knee, would he be dead? None of us really know the answer to that, but it begs the question. Biases spring from racism, institutionally and personally.

Implicit bias is about racism. If we truly care about fixing racism, leaders need to directly state and confront the issue. But first we need to acknowledge that it exists.

There are other high-profile cases involving white police officers killing black individuals. But we need to be cautious about assigning race as the root cause to all of the incidents. As sure as Dr. Gaddis breathes, he has no doubt that race played a role in all of these incidents involving police. And the narrative in the media will have you believe that white cops spend a majority of their workday killing unarmed black people. It's simply not true when you break down the actual data. Would it surprise you if I told you that 25 percent of those killed by police are black, and 50 percent of those killed by police are white?[*]

Cops kill more white people than black people. Those who argue in support of cops will rest their case on that fact alone. However, when you break down the demographics, it tells a more complex story. The black community only makes up 13 percent of the US population yet represents 25 percent of police killings. Now we are onto something. But what? There is an absolute disparity, and we are back to concluding that cops kill more blacks. But then we add in another layer of complexity. Blacks are 13 percent of the population, but commit at least 50 percent of the murders and other violent crimes according to FBI data.[†]

---

[*] *The Washington Post*, "Number of people shot to death by the police in the United States from 2017 to 2021, by race," Statista, accessed October 20, 2021. statista.com/statistics/585152/people-shot-to-death-by-us-police-by-race.

[†] "Arrests by Race and Ethnicity, 2016," 2016 Crime in the United States, Criminal Justice Information Services Division, FBI, accessed October 20, 2021. ucr.fbi.gov/crime-in-the-u.s/2016/crime-in-the-u.s.-2016/topic-pages/tables/table-21.

According to Statista, cops kill one thousand people on aver-age per year. And most of those shootings are justified—that is, in self-defense or in the process of protecting the life of another. But some are not justified. And some are so convoluted that no one can agree. As the verdict was being announced in the trial of George Floyd, a sixteen-year-old African American female was shot and killed by a Columbus, Ohio, police officer. The girl was attempting to stab two other people with a knife when the officer approached. She was armed with a knife and trying to kill some-one, and the police officer shot her to stop her. Was it justified? There was public outrage that yet another black person was killed by a white police officer. Had the knife wielding person been white, this probably wouldn't have made headlines. Does the fact that she's sixteen make a difference to you?

A police officer in Chicago was alerted to gunfire and located a person with a gun in a dark alley. The cop chased the offender and gave commands to drop the gun. The offender turned abruptly toward the officer, and the officer fired, killing him. When the officer went to render aid, he observed that it was a young man. The cop reacted by burying his face in his hands and becoming emotional. That young man was Adam Toledo, and he was a thir-teen-year-old Hispanic American. The video footage showed that Toledo tossed the gun less than one second before the officer pulled the trigger. It was 2:30 a.m., and Toledo had just fired a weapon at a car, and the officer located him and chased him. The officer saw the gun in his hand and made a split-second decision in a dark alley in the middle of the night. Was it justified?

In both of these instances, the offenders were juveniles. Does that make it more aggravating? It doesn't for me because a knife or a gun in the hand of a juvenile kills just the same as if it were in the hand of an adult.

There are nearly sixty million police encounters per year, and one thousand of these result in someone killed by a police officer.* That makes your odds of getting killed by the police one in sixty thousand. That should at the very least convince you that cops aren't cold-blooded killers. But one unjustified shooting is too many. And any police action that is based on race is unacceptable. But I want to make sure that we are all open to dissecting data so we can get as close to the truth as humanly possible. You may *feel* that these police actions are rooted in racism, but sometimes feelings get in the way of facts. Naturally, if we uncover any police officer using their power to harm a person solely because of their skin color, accountability must be swift and vigorous. We must be open to the reality that racism exists and determine if actions are rooted in bias. But we must also be willing to concede to the fact that many of these police actions are a result of people committing violence (cause) and an officer doing their job to stop them (effect).

---

* *The Washington Post*, "Number of people shot to death by the police in the United States from 2017 to 2021, by race," Statista, accessed October 1, 2021. statista.com/statistics/585152/people-shot-to-death-by-us-police-by-race.

CHAPTER SIX

GOOD APPLES

The police profession is currently in crisis because of the seemingly endless headlines that report police misconduct. There aren't enough hours in a news cycle to showcase the excellent service police officers provide to their citizens on a daily basis. I know this as sure as I am breathing. If you are rolling your eyes, perhaps you were the unfortunate recipient of a traffic citation or other incident of misfortune. Even so, I believe the majority of the police officers you encounter are polite and professional even when enforcing the law. Like your own profession, there are only a small percentage of police officers that skew the perspective with bad behavior or a bad attitude.

Despite the overwhelming majority of good police officers, it is the negative encounters we experience or read about that shape our viewpoint about the entire profession. There are nearly sixty million police contacts yearly, and the vast majority have a peaceful outcome. Those contacts range from answering a 9-1-1 call to assisting a motorist and everything in between. The majority of calls are uneventful and don't make headlines or a police report. And more often than you might think, officers do a remarkable job. Having been in an executive position in my police department for eleven years, I have been fortunate to receive phone calls, letters, and social media messages from hundreds of people who have taken the time to reach out and advise me of incidents where one of my officers went far above the call of duty. These stories sometimes leave me in awe.

I was driving my squad car past an east-side elementary school during dismissal. Some kids lingering in the crosswalk saw my uniform and ran up to say hello. One child seemed eager to get my attention and worked his way through the other kids to the window of my squad car and said, "Look at my coat!" I admired his winter coat and told him so. He replied, "A police officer bought it for me." Puzzled, I asked him which police officer, but he just shrugged his shoulders and ran away. I flagged down the teacher who was herding the kids, and she offered that the same officer stops by every morning to wave to the kids and noted that the student had a thin and ratty coat. She said the officer showed up on one of the mornings and handed the child a new coat. The teacher said the boy tells anyone who will listen about his new coat that the police officer bought him. I figured out who that officer was, and as you can imagine, he was uncomfortable with the praise I bestowed upon him. He said, "It's easier for me to take an ass-chewing than a compliment." As absurd as that sounds, I get it.

This episode made me reflect upon the many altruistic acts performed by my fellow officers that I had witnessed over the years and realize there were many similar, but untold stories. It's extremely contradictory to ask people to talk about acts of kindness they've performed because the mere fact that it's altruistic means they seek no recognition.

One officer tells the story of transporting a female to jail who was arrested for retail theft. As it turns out, she was stealing school supplies for her daughter because she could not afford to buy them. A jail officer sought out the list of needed supplies, bought them, and delivered them to the mother.

An officer responded to a call to find a family of six with only one bed in their apartment. The kids were sleeping with blankets on the apartment floor, so the officer donated a bed frame, mattress, and bedding from her own home to the family in need.

Two officers responded to a home where a distraught family had just witnessed their dog get hit by a car. The dog had taken its last breath, and the officers knew they couldn't leave the family in their grieving state, so they retrieved a blanket, wrapped the dog, and helped the kids write goodbye letters and place them with the dog for burial.

After taking a report from an elderly woman whose window-mounted air conditioner was stolen, the responding officers purchased another one and installed it for her.

But my favorite story left me breathless. An ex-prostitute with a drug habit was living on government aid in a housing project. She finally left the complex and went to rehab, never to return to that life again. A police officer privately funded her stay in rehab because he believed that she could turn her life around.

The nature of a police officer's job is to respond when people have been victimized or are at their worst. While this is the part of the job that tends to wear on officers, it also provides opportunities to make a difference—the very reason most of them enter this profession. There are countless other stories of purchasing coats for those who were cold, buying and delivering groceries and hot meals to those who were hungry, and replacing items for those who have been victimized. They do it not because they are police officers, but because they are human beings who instinctively extend their hand to help someone else in need.

We only hear about police officers who tarnish the badge and abuse their position of authority, and yes, we must shine the light in those dark places. The reality is that the majority of officers are reflections of the acts I've described. They use their power for good and like true heroes, prefer to do so when no one is watching and expecting nothing in return.

Right after I announced my retirement, I received this email from one of my officers: "I have to say thank you . . . to you! When you became Chief, you helped push a new era where it was ok to go above and beyond in helping people. We're blessed to have a job that pays well and we often cross paths with people that don't have much. I used to do things for people and not tell anyone. When you became Chief, we all felt a new vibe where I think we all felt more comfortable doing things for people. The culture changed at APD."

I will save this email forever so I am reminded that officers did appreciate being given the autonomy to be human. And I know they will continue these acts of altruism long after my tenure.

When I was appointed chief, I met with every group of new recruits. I used that time to share with them my vision and mission for our department, which included bringing their whole selves to work. We are a paramilitary organization, and we dress the same and have a formal chain of command, but that's where the uniformity stops. Every person who wears a badge is a human being made up of failures and fears that have shaped their lives. I tell the officers that I don't want a police force that borrows power from their position. I want a department of people who can bring their compassion, humor, empathy, and (gasp) vulnerability. I tell them I don't care whom they love, whom they voted for, whom they worship, etc. I only care that they bring their authentic selves to this job as they protect our community from harm. Cops need to be given permission to drop the "mirrored sunglasses and attitude" persona because bringing their skills and talents with their own individuality will make them better officers. Cops are human beings stitched up of flaws and good intentions—and so are most of the citizens they serve. When we focus on our similarities, we get better outcomes. I messed up a lot of things over the years, but this is what I needed to get right.

When I made the decision to retire, I understood the juxtaposition of policing and the polarizing views, but I knew that the officers in my department weren't to blame for the crisis in policing. They weren't making negative headlines. Certainly there have been incidents of misconduct by my cops, and I believe unequivocally there are officers who should not possess a badge. I have terminated five police officers in my tenure, and three got their jobs back because the union fought and won. None of these cases involved excessive force or an unlawful shooting, but the misconduct was enough for me to determine that these officers should not have the privilege of possessing a badge.

My decision to leave the department has a lot to do with the note the officer wrote me. There were many similar messages from officers that made me realize I had achieved what I set out to do: to alter the culture for the better. I know my department is better than I found it, and it occurred to me that I could have a greater impact on my beloved profession by consulting for other police departments. My intent is to use my voice to offer what I've learned about preventing and dealing with mass shootings, and to help other agencies live up to the nobility of policing.

CHAPTER SEVEN

FEAR IS A LIAR

I don't scare easily, and as I reflect back on my formative years, I'm sure it's because I beat grown men at billiards and practically raised myself on a pirate ship. I morphed from a bossy kid into a confident adult on what appeared to be a normal path—if you didn't know the backstory. All those Slim Jims caught up with me, and I turned chubby in junior high. Fortunately, I was funny, and because kids are drawn to the class clown, I had a lot of friends. These years were entirely different from my Christian elementary school years. Then, I felt lonely and isolated because I never fit in. What's more, the demographics of my private school differed from the kids in my neighborhood and the patrons at the club. I didn't understand classism at the time, but I knew there was an absolute disparity between the houses of my Aurora Christian friends and my own. Mom dropped me off for school in the morning in a green Ford Pinto with a cream primer-colored driver's door. My face grew hot with shame when she pulled into the circle with all the other shiny cars to drop me off. I exited her car as fast as I could in hopes that no one would associate me with it.

Plus, I felt as though I was leading two lives as a parochial student by day and a pool shark by night. Mom loved the Lord Jesus Christ and did a great job building my spiritual foundation, taking me to church on Sundays and Bible school in the summer. But Dad and J.C. weren't on the best terms, so while Dad paid the big price tag to send me to a private religious school, he rolled his eyes at religion as an institution. He was a science fanatic, so when I was with Dad, he educated me about the cosmos and evolution; meanwhile, in school I learned that God created Heaven and Earth. I carried a Bible with notched tabs on the side, so I could easily find the chapter and verse to contradict what Dad had told me. We had deep discussions about religion and how he believed it was man-made. Yet I believed in God because I was nervous about being banished to the fiery depths of Hell. I felt conflicted about evolutionary theory and the universe given what my teachers and the Bible had told me. Looking back, Dad's perspective made more sense. Creating woman from the rib of man sounded a bit preposterous compared with the notion of cells multiplying to form human life—not to mention the latter had been proven by scientists. My formative years felt as if I were living in two distinct universes: either Dad's version was right, or it was wrong. Since he spent most of his time philosophizing about this stuff on a barstool, I gave credence to my teachers at school.

One day in second grade, I lost the charm to my necklace. I was so distraught because my grandma from Norway had sent it to me, so my teacher offered to help me find it. She took me by the hand and told me to close my eyes. I thought perhaps she was going to ask me to visualize my steps during the day to determine where I'd lost the charm. Instead, she prayed: "God will bring your necklace back to you. God will provide. In Jesus's name, Amen." And then she sent me back to my seat. I told Dad, only to hear him laugh the kind of laugh that leads to coughing. Maybe it was from the cigarettes. Nevertheless, he had made fun of my teacher's prayer and asked me whether I'd considered problem solving and looking for the charm instead of praying about it. The more he laughed, the angrier I got. But I realized quickly that I was angry because he made me feel stupid for praying to God to help me find my charm. He said I should have stuck with my instinct to retrace my steps, work backward from where I noticed it gone, and search for it methodically. I cried angrily because I knew he was right. I felt judged by him, and that feeling was enough to shape me into a person who hates feeling stupid. I never found the charm, and that confirmed for me that praying for something to happen (or not happen) isn't necessarily the right answer. My mom thought differently. She believed that God would always provide, and her unwavering faith in mankind and religion shaped me in a way that smoothed out the jagged edge of pessimism that my dad instilled in me. She believed that everything happened for a reason, and our fate rested in the Lord's will. Dad only believed in things he could see and understand. Mom trusted everyone, and Dad trusted no one.

Because of my parents' sprawling differences, I grew to understand and respect that people held different beliefs. I understood that beliefs and values, be they religion, politics, or ice-cream flavors, dictate how people behave in the world. My life was shaped by these conflicting beliefs, so I spent time collecting data and determining which version of the truth made more sense. I felt judged by Dad for believing in God, but if I swayed toward his critical thinking, I battled with fear and shame for not believing. I didn't realize until much later in life how my parents' polarizing beliefs forced me to gather evidence and form my own opinions rather than blindly follow what someone told me. I had these mutually exclusive beliefs about religion that I learned to navigate. Now in my late forties, I understand how my belief system was forged. On a line with the predominant political parties at each end of the spectrum, my beliefs fall squarely in the middle. I'm that dot that won't commit to either side. I'm not liberal, but I'm not conservative. I don't identify with a party because I vote on single issues. I am pro-choice. I own guns. I love money, but I also love giving it away to those who need it. I believe in feeding the hungry, but I despise those who take advantage of the system. I'm a goddamn mishmash of all the beliefs.

Aside from being a critical thinker, one of the greatest gifts I received from Dad was an immunity to being laughed at. Dad thought everything was funny, and when he started laughing (either with or at me), he made me laugh, too. He often pointed out stumbles, not in a way that was cruel but in a way that highlighted the absurdity. This attitude morphed into learning to laugh at myself when I did something stupid or made a mistake. I discovered throughout my life that if I learned to laugh at myself the loudest, it drowned out anyone else laughing at me.

I was secretly relieved when my parents sat me down to tell me they couldn't afford to send me to private school anymore, and I'd

have to start sixth grade at public school. I had grown tired of praying for everything at school, and by that time, I subscribed to Dad's
mindset of getting off my ass to make something happen. The irony
of Dad's giving me this advice from a barstool is not lost on me.
My neighborhood friends went to public school, and because we all
had the same-sized house on the same block, I didn't feel ashamed
or less-than. When I walked into my sixth-grade elementary class
as the new kid, I felt as if I owned the place, as if I belonged. I had
found my tribe, and for some reason, I was confident and fearless.
As the chubby funny kid, I quickly made friends.

My junior high years were spent with public school kids who
had much of the same dysfunction in their families. As a rat pack
of kids who were largely unsupervised, we engaged in nuisance
activities that never quite reached the level of hardcore criminal
acts. We climbed onto the roof of the neighborhood school to
smoke cigarettes and played lots of ding-dong ditch. The other
kids drank alcohol, but I refused because I was afraid that if I tried
it, I would become an alcoholic like Dad. In those early teen years,
I craved rules and boundaries but had none. As my friends around
me became more immersed in bad behavior, I tried to fit in, but I
couldn't do it. I didn't want to be home because I couldn't handle
my parents fighting, but I didn't want to be away because I worried
about leaving Mom alone when Dad was drunk. I lived in constant
fear that she was going to die in a car accident because Dad had
no problem driving drunk with us in the car. If I called home and
Mom didn't answer the phone, it was my routine to call emergency
rooms to see if she was there. That phase lasted about a year. I
obviously didn't want to be with my parents, but I also started to
realize I didn't fit in with the other junior high kids. Because I had

developed a pretty assertive personality—thanks to hanging in the bar—I had no problem opting out of bad decisions unapologetically. In an odd way, my Christian school education that I thought I despised was the thing that kept me on track. The commandments and parables had lessons attached to them, and whether you believed in God or not, those virtuous stories were powerful. I am certain my moral compass was honed because of my religious and rule-abiding formative years. Without that religious education, I would likely have stayed in that group of friends, of which three are dead and one is serving a life sentence for murder.

When I got to high school, I met Carrie, Beth, Dawn, and Shannon. We all went to the same junior high together, but we didn't cross paths much. Carrie's dad, Mr. Fisher, was a science teacher at our school, so she couldn't be too naughty because he and his teacher friends were always watching. Carrie soon became my best friend, and she pulled me into her friend group, where I remain to this day. I slept over at Carrie's house one night during our freshman year and didn't leave her house for the next three years. These friends were different from my junior high group because they were studious rule followers with a streak of rebellion. But their kind of rebellion was the normal kind and not the kind that would result in a rap sheet—although we did have an encounter with the cops one Friday night when we got pulled over for being out past curfew. They let us go but not before they took our McDonald's bag with double cheeseburgers and fresh fries that we had just secured from the drive-thru. That was an abuse of power that, like other more brutal police actions, was "overlooked" at the time. I'm sure those confiscated McDonald's bags are still in the evidence locker at the station.

The good influence of my friends, who cared about their grades and had dreams of college and careers, surely saved me. During my sophomore year of high school, Carrie's parents arranged for a family portrait of their immediate family, which included her parents, their four kids, and me. They included me in every family vacation and paid for me without saying a word, never making me feel like a freeloader. When Carrie and I were caught sneaking out of the house—with her older sister's aluminum can booby trap crashing down from above the door—we both were grounded. I didn't quite understand the significance of someone else's family welcoming me into it until I became an adult. When I was well into my policing career, I realized that a kid going down the wrong road could be saved by one person who cared enough to invest in her.

The Fisher family gave me stability when I didn't have it at my own home. Things were so bad between Mom and Dad that she became more depressed while he turned to the liquor cabinet to quiet his mind and numb his reality. I distanced myself from both of them because it seemed to me that at fifteen years old, I was the only sane one. They never once told me to come home during those years. As a parent, I cannot fathom one of my kids leaving my home at fifteen and not returning. At the time, I couldn't comprehend the gravity of moving out (even though I never declared I was doing so). In my mind, I was just sleeping over at my best friend's house. Permanently. I loved Mom and was so protective of her, but I somehow understood that I had to get out of the dysfunction.

Despite this odd and informal exchange of custody, I never lost the confidence I'd formed as a pool shark in the bar. I shed my Slim Jim baby fat just before my senior year and became even more sure of myself. Inexplicably, I always felt confident and in charge throughout my life. Even when I was scared, I tapped the reservoir of bravery inside me. I don't know where the bravery came from, but I was never afraid to try and fail. I'm still not afraid. During my senior year of high school, I walked into an audition for the lead role in the spring musical after never having stepped foot on a real stage in my life. I joined the school newspaper and asked if I could have my own column. I decided that I was going to be a cop, so I interviewed for the position of police cadet at the Aurora Police Department—and got the job. I graduated from high school in June and started working at the police department in July. I told my friends I was going to be chief of police one day, but I was just kidding. I swear. At that time, there were no women of rank at all, so I was being absurd. I also have told people that had I not gone into policing, I would have been a cast member on *Saturday Night Live*. I find myself hilarious and can rock a Kristen Wiig impression but have yet to find anyone who thinks I'm as funny as I do. My point is that neither *SNL* nor police chief was in the cards for me.

Despite Dad's demons, he glorified the job of policing for me. He'd tell me stories of calls to which he responded, and I knew he approached policing the same way he parented me (if you can call it parenting)—with problem solving and logic. For everything that was wrong in my childhood, I came out the other side with tremendous resiliency. The resilience and confidence I have doesn't always compute into the way others see me. When I put on my uniform for the first time, I realized that my unintimidating stature of five feet, four inches and 120 pounds soaking wet did not lend the physical prowess to back up my fearlessness. I got to this place because my bravery reservoir contained an "act as if" mindset. Every time I was scared, I pretended to be brave. This likely came from acting like my homelife was normal like everyone else's at my private school as well as being left to fend for myself.

GETTING COMFORTABLE WITH BEING AFRAID

When I inhaled courage and exhaled fear, my physiology began to change. Aristotle's philosophy that virtues are derived from action most likely resonated with me because Dad had always told me to get off my ass. I subscribed to Aristotle's and Malcolm Gladwell's claim that habit and repetition build excellence. The more you do the thing you want to become better at, the better you become. Extending this philosophy to fear, the more you lean into fear and do the thing that scares you, the more courageous you become. At the club, I practiced being tough when inebriated men cornered me in the hallway to the restroom. If they got close enough for me to smell the sweet, sour booze on their breath, I'd warn them not to take one step closer or else they'd get a pool cue where the sun doesn't shine. They'd laugh and stumble away. I remember a few times when I was so shaken that I had to recover in a bathroom stall to calm myself. When Lenny (the guy who shined the floors at the club) molested me at twelve years old, I pushed him off me and told Mom. Later that evening, I awoke to a loud argument and found Dad in the kitchen stuffing his gun into his cowboy boot. He was drunk and had a mind to kill Lenny. I pled with him not to kill the man, but Dad left anyway. I don't know what happened that night, but I was so relieved when Dad came home hours later and passed out. I was even more relieved when I saw Lenny alive at the club the next week. Dad didn't kill him, but I had to go to counseling and point on a doll to where Lenny had touched me. I was annoyed with Dad for causing me more fear than Lenny had.

Fear was not a new emotion to me as a cadet. Maybe I learned to manage my fear early on. For one, I felt a lot of fear when it came to Dad's unpredictability when he drank. On many occasions, I was in the car with Dad when he was too drunk to drive. He was in many accidents, but only about half of them were with me in the car. The scariest one was when he drove off the road and into a tree after we left the house of a fellow crony from the club. My parents dragged me to all their friends' homes while they drank and played poker, and I would fall asleep on top of all the coats that were piled high in a bedroom until it was time to go home. Dad carried me sleepily to the car where I would be too terrorized by his driving to fall back asleep. To this day, I still remember the feeling of riding in the car with my drunk driver dad. He had a habit of swerving off the road or into the center lane of an oncoming vehicle. Despite the sheer terror, Mom and I always got into the car because it was futile to fight with him. One night, Mom tried to get the keys from him, and instead of turning them over, he decided to teach her a lesson for even suggesting he wasn't okay to operate a vehicle. I'll never forget that night as he wove in and out of traffic down Hill Avenue as I screamed and pleaded for him to stop.

When I was fourteen and alone with Dad on a drunken day, I took the keys and told him I would be driving home. The only time I had driven his car was when he put me in the driver's seat and told me to cruise the grocery store parking lot, when I was thirteen. He said it was a skill I needed to have, so I used that logic on him and got in the driver's seat. I was terrified of driving in traffic because I had never done it. I acknowledged that I was scared and took a deep breath, pushing through the discomfort and scary stuff and getting us home safe. All those experiences in the car with Dad had elicited physical fear. Over my police career, I have felt afraid many times, but interestingly enough, I have rarely felt fear when it came to my physical well-being. I never worried about dying on the job because I thought I was bulletproof. Maybe that was a result of not yet being conscious of my own mortality; or maybe that's the result of growing up in chaos. I'm not exactly sure why I was more afraid of being physically harmed by my dad's driving than being a cop on the street. Ironically, responding to bar fights or gunshots never made me feel scared. The only times I have felt fear had nothing to do with physical harm but more so of failing or falling short. Over the years, I pretended to have a "You can't hurt me" attitude, and I have been pretty successful in believing that lie. The truth is none of us are bulletproof when it comes to our physical or emotional safety. We are all human beings with emotions, and even those of us who think we can build a fortress to protect us from feeling are mistaken. The things we fear are different for each of us. Some fear death while others welcome it as a bridge to the afterlife.

Some people fear failure or ridicule, not physical harm. Fear will keep you frozen in place because it's human nature to avoid pain, so why do anything that might risk causing it? Why connect with another human being when the risk of being betrayed or hurt is a possible outcome? Why proclaim a new and radical idea and invite criticism or judgment? No matter the source of fear, leaning into the thing that scares you is the remedy to overcoming it. Whether it be taking the keys from my dad or deciding to do something that might open me up to ridicule, just one action forward was the beginning of overcoming the fear. When I talk with others who decide not to take risks, they often express that the fear of criticism keeps them from moving forward. Because action creates movement, and movement creates momentum, soon you might find yourself on the other side of fear, where courage and confidence are waiting.*

No matter what it is you are afraid of, that fear dictates how you move about the world. I have discovered a remedy for fear, and I call it the "Litmus Test for Courage." No matter what decision I am about to make or risk I'm about to embark on, I ask myself, "What is the worst thing that could happen?" Some people think I'm inviting bad juju or negative energy into the equation by inviting the worst possible scenario, but I disagree. I literally come up with a devastating outcome, and I sit with that for a while. When contemplating applying for a new position or determining whether to publish this book, I go to the worst-case scenario. In applying for a new position, the worst thing is that I might not get it. When I applied for the position of Chicago Police Superintendent, I decided that the worst thing that could happen was *getting* the job (no kidding). When deciding to publish the words you are reading, the worst thing that could happen is that you hate this book, and I've wasted your time. When deciding to become a police officer, I understood the worst thing that could happen was that I don't come home at the end of my shift.

---

* It's important to note that moving through the world without fear of physical harm is a privilege. One thing I have learned from listening to people of color is they are always aware of the threat of physical harm at the hands of a police officer. So leaning into that fear may not make sense in the way I'm suggesting.

As you can see, these outcomes are vastly different. Deciding to become a police officer means facing the stark reality that it might be life threatening. But almost everything else is not that deep. If you hate this book, I am deeply sorry, but we are both going to be just fine. Once you sit with the worst potential outcome, decide if you are willing to accept that outcome. I find that making peace with the worst thing that can happen gives me clarity. Allowing yourself to prepare for the worst possible thing that might happen and then accepting it gives you the burst of courage to proceed. Naturally, if you decide you are unwilling to accept the worst outcome, you might decide not to move forward. And that's okay. By the way, I have found that we often catastrophize, and the worst thing that could possibly happen often doesn't. Fear is a liar, so face it head on.

CHAPTER EIGHT

COURAGE TO BE VULNERABLE

I've always felt more excited than scared when embarking on something new and different in my life. Beginning my career as a sworn officer was no exception. I loved being a cadet, but those years were just stepping stones to get me closer to being a real cop. I graduated from the academy with honors and passed the firearms course with expert classification. I felt mighty despite my small stature, but I still had to overcome some antiquated thinking from my superiors.

All new police officers must go through field training after graduating from the academy. The program is four months long, and a different field training officer, or FTO, is assigned each month. At the end of each week, I had to sit down with my FTO and the lieutenant to go over my progress. In the third month of the program, my FTO advised the lieutenant that I was doing well and flying through the program. The lieutenant skimmed through the paperwork and addressed the training officer as if I wasn't in the room: "That's fine that she's doing well, but have you got her into a fight? Can she hold her own?" I remained silent, and my training officer paused for a moment. "Lieutenant, she has actually diffused many situations so she didn't have to fight. That is exactly what we want to see in a recruit." I could have jumped out of my chair and kissed that man. In the early '90s, when I joined the force, if you didn't fight, you couldn't possibly be a good cop. I had made it through my life up to that point without getting into fights, so the concept was a bit foreign to me. Surprisingly, I made it through the program without punching people, but I still had to endure being underestimated, a recurring theme throughout my career.

I was released from the field training program with high marks, so when I hit the street as a solo officer, I was more than ready. For the first year on the job, I pretended to be tough, and I talked a big game. I walked around with my oversized gun belt and flung around my authority by borrowing power from my position. I gave orders and lectured people when they broke the law, and the colorful world I had come to know morphed into black and white. I categorized those who broke the law as "criminals," and every encounter became us versus them. I was part of an army of law enforcers, and it was my responsibility to make sure that everyone obeyed the law. I felt as though I needed to prove myself to other officers and to those who commented on my petite stature. I thought that by acting fierce and commanding, I would overcome the perception that I was weak. I morphed into a person I did not recognize, yet I reconciled this transformation as necessary to fulfill my dream of being a cop. I had no choice but to act like the other cops, and if that meant changing my personality, I was willing to do it. Who we are by default is difficult to reprogram, so I started to feel like an imposter hiding behind a uniform. And it was exhausting.

The culture of an organization is like a living, breathing organism. We spend most of our time synchronizing our actions and emulating social cues so we don't draw attention to ourselves. This is especially true when we enter a new environment like a new job or a foreign place for the first time. If you are new, the last thing you want to do is draw attention to yourself or be too different, so you find ways to adapt and blend inconspicuously so as not to reveal too quickly how weird you actually are. This is a survival technique, and it's not always a bad thing because it allows time for us to transition into a new environment incrementally. It's very primitive because adapting is what we are hardwired to do. The more we admire the profession or the institution, the more desperate we are to fit in.

The problem is that when we focus all our energy on adapting, we lose our personhood and fade into the background. Desperate to fit in, we override our belief system, and we do things we wouldn't normally do out of fear of ridicule. We have the desire to fit in, and if we don't constantly fight to go against the grain, we will find ourselves ingrained in something that is unrecognizable. We do this in the boardroom and in social situations. We try so hard to become part of the in-group that we overlook things that would normally be offensive. Nervously laughing at a racist joke or ignoring an overt act of injustice are small but dangerous ways we adapt to our surroundings in desperation of being accepted. Over time, we discover that we've lost ourselves, and we aren't quite sure how it happened.

Life has a way of handing out much-needed lessons, and mine was provided to me in my second year on the job. I decided to do some traffic enforcement, so I parked my squad car tucked back behind a building so I could be stealthy while watching a stop sign. This hiding place was like shooting fish in a barrel because people always ran the stop sign, and I could fulfill the lieutenant's expectations of writing tickets. I watched the stop sign for only a few minutes before I had my first violator. The car blew through the intersection without even trying to roll, so I hit my lights, and the stop was on. This was my favorite part of the job. I loved the rush of adrenaline I got when I flipped the switch, and the "cherries" spun on top of the squad car. It's also a moment of data collection for a cop. We pay close attention to the vehicle occupants and note if there are any sudden movements inside the car. I am always amused by those who quickly reach across their body to buckle their seatbelts as if we don't see them doing it.

In this case, the driver hesitated and didn't pull over right away, so we continued around a curve until his vehicle came to a stop. I called in the license plate and vehicle information to dispatch, and I exited my squad to approach the driver. I made contact with him, and he handed me his ID card. I told him why I stopped him and said I would be back. He wasn't belligerent or uncooperative. He didn't say anything in response to my advising him that I watched him run the stop sign. He simply provided me with what I asked for, and as I walked to my squad, I glanced back to make sure he was staying seated in his car. I started to run his identity through the mobile computer in my squad when the computer "dinged" to notify me that he had several warrants and was flagged for being "armed and dangerous." I looked up to see him bolt from the car. I instinctively leaped out of my squad, and the chase was on. It must have looked ridiculous for a five-foot-four baby cop with a bouncing pony tail to be sprinting after a six-foot-three muscleman, but I wasn't considering that. All I could think about was catching him, so I ran as fast as I could. As the gap between us closed, I recalled thinking, "What am I going to do when I catch him?"

So, I formulated a plan to pounce and tackle him to the ground, then handcuff him. I got within three feet and sprung on him with Tigger agility and grabbed his shoulders, but he didn't fall. His footing wasn't the least bit affected by my acrobatic feat. I didn't have a plan B because it never occurred to me that physics would thwart plan A. I never made a conscious decision to hang on to him—it just happened. And for reasons I still don't understand, he kept running, and I hung on tight. So as I was riding this guy's back through the backyards of a neighborhood on the east side of Aurora, my tough-guy act fell away. I said to him, "We both know you could really hurt me if you wanted to. But you won't—because it won't increase your street cred given my obvious proportion. And it certainly won't help my reputation among my fellow officers. So let's just end this, and I'll arrest you for your warrants, which is inevitable sooner or later anyway. I won't charge you with fleeing, and we'll call it a day."

I'm sure I didn't sound as articulate, but that was the gist. And right after I spoke to him, he stopped. Just like that, he stopped abruptly. I slid down his back and handcuffed him with no issue whatsoever. As we walked back to my squad car, I asked him, "Why did you stop?" He replied, "No cop has ever just talked to me." I stopped and looked at him. He didn't expound on his statement, but I knew exactly what he meant, and his words filled me with confusion and clarity at the same time. He ran from my traffic stop. He started this negative encounter, but his words suggested that I had controlled the outcome. He never displayed a weapon, but I understood that his physical stature put me at a tactical disadvantage, and I knew that my level of force would be justified if I could articulate that I felt my life was in danger. I don't know what caused me to use words instead of the other tactical options on my belt, but it worked. The greatest tool we possess to alter the outcome of an encounter is our human interaction, and instinctively, I knew that. In that moment, I understood what I now believe is the key to policing and every other human interaction: talk to people as though they are worthy of your respect and humanity. Even when someone is breaking the law, treat them with dignity. Unless you are looking down the barrel of a gun or at the blade of a knife, use the power of human connection to find common ground.

This epiphany was happening while I walked him back to my squad car, and my thoughts were interrupted. "You dropped something back there," he said. I reached down on my gun belt and noticed a gaping vacancy where my police radio used to be. Apparently, it bounced out of its holder while I was riding his back across the fence lines. Then we walked together so he could show me where I had dropped it—no kidding! I picked it up and said, in my most confident voice over the air, "Subject in custody."

I wish I could report that this interaction between the big guy and me caused him to change his ways and become a model citizen. Unfortunately, he continued his life of crime, and I ran into him many times throughout my career, but he never gave me a problem. He gave other cops a problem—but not me. In fact, if I showed up on a call with him, he would speak only to me. I think of this dynamic like cops and robbers. People are going to continue to break the law, and cops are going to try and catch them. But the best police officers I know don't take it personally and practice humanity in their interactions. The ideal outcome is that no one is hurt. And in these times where citizens are questioning whether police officers value human life, humanity matters more than anything else.

The best officers I know are the ones who value human life and show empathy for those they encounter. Cops have to understand that each crime victim is going through a traumatic experience. Even if an officer has taken several burglary reports in one day, it is still a profound feeling of violation to each of the victims. The officers who understand and empathize are already practicing the concept of treating the person and not the crime. Since crime victims comprise most of our encounters, they are left with a positive feeling about the police despite the crime against them. That means the cops are compassionate in the process of doing their jobs. It's no different from providing great customer service to clients. Cops need to remember that our citizens are the customers.

The real secret sauce is having the courage to be vulnerable. The truth is, when I was riding on that guy's back, I was terrified. I had no clue where I was, and even if I had known, I didn't have a radio to call for backup. The only tactic left was to acknowledge that he could overpower me. It was vulnerable, and it was a risk, but it was the truth. After that incident, I started confronting my fears and vulnerabilities and being honest about them. Instead of attempting to emulate the tough cops with attitude, I started being me. My tough-guy persona wasn't working for me, and I began to understand that it might put me more at risk on the street. I began bringing my authentic personality to my job, and as a consequence, I started enjoying my job. I learned that when you treat people with dignity and respect and never look down on them (even when they are literally lying in the gutter), they will likely cooperate or even help you. It seemed that the cranky cops got that way because of the conflict they created, and once I figured out that I didn't have to be authoritative and tough all the time, I didn't feel drained from all the energy expended by always being at odds with everyone. I was still the same bossy pants as before, but it was different because command presence can coexist with kindness.

I became a more successful police officer because I could determine the best outcome in a situation by listening and problem solving. I stopped trying to be what I believed I was supposed to be and started being exactly who I was. I diffused situations with humor, and I didn't withhold compassion like I thought I was supposed to do. I originally held the belief that my male colleagues didn't think women belonged in policing, and because I didn't want to appear weak, I felt as though I couldn't be kind. Most of my insecurities were self-imposed, and I thought I had to prove I was tough, but once I figured out that I didn't need to alter my personality, everything changed. I was me. Over time, I began to notice the police officers who were also really good at communicating were the most successful ones. I also came to know the officers who arrived on scene, created more havoc, and agitated rather than calmed people; I tried to keep them as far away from my call as possible.

When police officers are given permission to use their humor, empathy, compassion, and individual talents while carrying out their duties, the job still gets done. In fact, it gets done better because authenticity and trust are the foundation of legitimacy. Who provides this permission? The answer is that we do, individually. Having the courage to behave in a way that is not the norm draws attention to us. If we can withstand the attention (and maybe even ridicule) yet still continue to do things differently, it gives permission for others to drop their façade and follow suit. A culture is made up of people, and it changes only when individuals assume the responsibility.

CHAPTER NINE

A DAB OF GUN OIL

It's hard to talk about personal responsibility without discussing one of the most controversial issues in the present day. I've grown up around guns. My dad kept his service revolver in the top drawer of his dresser in his bedroom. He knew I knew it was there, and he told me I wasn't allowed to touch it. The fact that I didn't harm myself is a miracle because I touched it a lot. When I was home alone, I opened his dresser drawer and wrapped my hand around the wooden grip. I remember the barrel being shiny as a result of his constant polishing. It was his routine to clean and polish his gun and his boots, and I relished in watching him take pride in both. The gun was so heavy in my hands, and I remember being surprised by the weight of it. Metaphorically, how fitting that an object that can eradicate a human life carries such weight. Each time I picked up his gun, I walked to the mirror with it, held it up to my eye to aim, and said, "Freeze, dirtbag." I could see my reflection in the mirror with the gun pointing back at me, and I felt so empowered. I never put my finger around the trigger because I understood cause and effect. I knew something bad would happen if I pointed it anywhere other than the mirror, but it was still reckless.

When I got hired as a cadet, the first thing they did was take us to the shooting range. As a result of my Charlie's Angel poses in the mirror with my dad's gun, I was immediately comfortable with the semiautomatic 9 mm Sig Sauer P228 that I held in my hand. Shooting was something that came natural to me, and I aced the targets almost every time.

I own only three guns: my duty firearm, a small off-duty 9 mm, and my dad's duty revolver—the same duty revolver I pointed into the mirror. Consequently, the same revolver he would use to kill himself.

I am not a gun enthusiast, but I work with many individuals who are. I like my gun, and I feel safer when I'm carrying one of them given the amount of gun violence on the streets, but I don't dab gun oil behind my ears. In fact, I probably would not own a gun if I weren't a cop. I carry my weapon off duty because I shudder at the thought of being unarmed in a situation where I could have used my firearm to stop a violent act. But that is the mindset of a cop. I'm confident in my abilities and in my mindset because it has been instilled in me. I'm not convinced that people who tote guns around with them everywhere have the training and mindset to put themselves in harm's way to stop a threat. We like to think we are that hero who would stop a shooter, but in the heat of the moment, many of us are not.

Unlike people who have arsenals in their homes, I never saw the point. There are people who are convinced that the government is going to come for their guns, and they need to be prepared to overthrow when that occurs. Gosh, I haven't heard one politician oppose gun ownership, but far be it from me to judge those who live in that realm. I am a person who respects the Constitution and the rule of law, and the right to keep and bear arms is one to which we must adhere. I have always been of the opinion that the law of the land is written and must be abided.

Like most things in life, we feel one way about a particular thing until something occurs that personally affects us. For me, it was the mass shooting in my city. When the events unfolded and we learned that the shooter *illegally* possessed the gun that he used to kill five people and shoot five of my officers, I was enraged. I was enraged at the system that allowed this man with a violent, criminal record to possess a firearm. Instantly, I changed course and found myself arguing with the constitutionalists who believe *anyone* is entitled to possess a gun.

Trever Wehner was the youngest victim of the mass shooting in my city. He was only twenty-one years old, and when I went to his funeral, his mother was touching him in the casket. I locked eyes with her, but she wouldn't even remember that happened because she was a shell of a human being standing over her son, whose life had been stolen by a monster. In that moment, the absurdity of the fight against gun legislation to prevent other monsters from stealing lives was so clear to me. Guns don't kill— people do. That's the argument, right? I agree that people kill, which is why we should make sure monsters disguised as people don't have access to guns. But my favorite rebuttal is that if guns were taken away, humans would find other ways to kill people. The vehicle analogy is amusing to me as well. There are people who drive a car into a crowd of victims with the intent to kill as many as possible, and we aren't banning cars. The anti-intellectualism in this example hurts my head. Correct, cars can be used to purposely kill people, but they were not created for that purpose. Since the trend of mass casualties by those driving cars into crowds, measures have been taken to prevent it. Bollards and physical barriers have been erected in areas that draw crowds of people. In my own city, we deploy dump trucks to block intersections so cars cannot pummel through and injure people. Why can't we set up some of the same "barriers" for gun owners? The mass shooter in my city didn't have to submit fingerprints to obtain the Firearm Owner's Identification Card that allowed him to purchase the weapon. Had he been fingerprinted, the felony conviction for domestic battery would have shown up, and he would have been denied the card. Had that happened, Trevor's mom wouldn't have to wake up every day without her son. Had that happened in many of these mass shootings that have become so commonplace, we might have been able to stop these monsters from getting a gun. So yes, by all means, we have the right to bear arms, but I doubt our forefathers predicted the invention of semiautomatic weapons that would be used to mass execute other human beings.

I am a legal gun owner with no intent to commit crimes against other people, and I have zero problem submitting to whatever it is you need me to do to ensure that I am not a risk to harm anyone. Most reasonable gun owners who aren't cops feel the same. Jesus, if we could stop these madmen from killing sprees by agreeing to submit to a background check and fingerprints, why wouldn't we? I'm not suggesting it's completely foolproof (just as some bad apple cops slip through the cracks), but it would significantly reduce the number of illegal guns placed in the palms of lunatics.

And for those who say we can't amend the Constitution, I have a few history lessons for you. The Eighteenth Amendment prohibited the sale of alcohol in order to "ameliorate poverty and other societal issues." That's a fancy way of saying that too many people were spending their hard-earned money on alcohol, and it was causing them some life trouble. This amendment led to a decline in alcohol consumption in the United States. But authorities were finding it difficult to enforce as people were cooking up moonshine in their bathtubs. Turns out, folks just couldn't live without their alcohol, so the Constitution was amended again. The Twenty-First Amendment repealed the prohibition.

I don't think I should have to remind anyone that owning a slave was a constitutional right. The document didn't contain the word "slave," but it received protections in the Constitution. The notorious three-fifths clause was the clever loophole that provided the South extra representation and extra votes. This prohibited Congress from outlawing the Atlantic slave trade for twenty years. Basically, the Constitution strengthened slavery, but was powerful enough to eventually abolish it.

When people ask me whom I would opt to have a meal with, living or dead, I always say our forefathers. I would bring all the mothers of the mass shooting victims with me. I bet each one of our Founding Fathers would be surprised by the technology that has surpassed the musket, and my guess is they would change their stance with this new information brought to their attention. And then everyone else would release their grip on gun laws, and just like there was a decline in alcohol consumption, I bet there would be a decline in mass shootings.

I'm never the smartest person in the room, but I have yet to hear an argument against gun legislation that moves me. I have people in my inner circle that I love and adore who fight with me frequently on this topic, and all they can say is that gun owners need to be free from government intrusion. And then I retort that sometimes the government has to step in because human beings need to be saved from themselves. Seat belts are a great example. Car crashes were killing people at a high rate, so the government swooped in and mandated seatbelts. Now people don't die as much. My friends then offer the same rebuttal: driving a car is not a constitutional right, but gun ownership is. Then I remind them of the Commerce Clause in the Constitution. Adherence to the rigid interpretation means that passing through states in automobiles is an act of interstate commerce. We argue this point, then we declare impasse and order tacos because everyone agrees on tacos. Ironically, we discuss the latest mass shooting and how crime is up while eating our tacos.

People with guns kill people. But for the grace of God, may no one you love dearly be in the Walmart, the movie theater, the place of worship, the school, the grocery store, the workplace (anywhere) when a person who shouldn't have a gun decides to erase their lives with the pull of a trigger. I am not advocating taking guns away from law-abiding citizens, but let's meet in the middle to ensure they don't get into the hands of people who are mentally ill or intending to do harm.

CHAPTER TEN

INNER BOSS

Becoming a leader has meant taking positions and making decisions that I felt were the right thing to do even if it meant upsetting people. Like my stance on guns, I have strong opinions that have been molded through my life experiences, and I've gotten comfortable sharing them. I was asked to speak to a leadership academy class where I offered my views on leadership and lessons learned, and when I was finished, a handsome man with a crisp, button-down shirt raised his hand and said, "I don't have a question—I have a comment: You should write a book."

I looked at him sideways and said, "Okay," but not confirming that I would actually take his suggestion. It was more of a confused okay. I didn't know this guy at all, so I appeased him, hoping we could move on to real questions. I went home that night and couldn't snuff out the little spark that he'd planted in my head. So I started writing and didn't stop. And that is how this book came to be. It never occurred to me that anything I said would be worth reading, but the guy in the nice shirt was certain about it. That meant at least one person would read it, so I decided I was already at an advantage.

When I made the decision to write this book, I reflected on the path that brought me to the top of my agency's organizational chart. I recall that certain traits of leadership emerged within me at a young age.

When I was a little girl, my two best friends lived in my neighborhood. On the days I didn't go with my dad to the club, Marcy, Heather, and I pretended to be the famous country music trio the Mandrell sisters: Barbara, Louise, and Irlene. They had their own Emmy Award–winning television show in the early 1980s where they sang together, and we girls were obsessed with them. We knew all the lyrics to their songs, and the three of us actually believed we *were* the Mandrell sisters. I was always Barbara. It was not up for negotiation. I organized the concerts atop my parents' red picnic table with the wobbly top on the patio, and I decided the set list. I introduced my sisters in front of the audience of empty lawn chairs: "My name is Barbara Mandrell, and we are the Mandrell sisters!" Marcy and Heather said in order, "I'm Louise" and "I'm Irlene." And they fell in line behind me as my backup girls. All was right with the world as we sang "Sleeping Single in a Double Bed" on my Mister Microphone, despite having no clue what those lyrics meant.

One day, Marcy suggested that we should rotate who got to be Barbara. She dared to say it wasn't fair that I always got to be Barbara and wondered why I was the boss. I couldn't believe it. In my mind, Marcy did not have what it took to organize the details. Not only that, but Barbara had the blondest hair of the sisters, and I had the blondest hair of my friends. And Barbara was the oldest sister, and I was older than Marcy and Heather. Then, Heather chimed in and complained how unfair it was that she always had to be Irlene, and she was tired of my being the boss. It was anarchy! I had lost control! They both dramatically took off their costume dresses draped over their shorts and tank tops and sat down on the picnic table stage. There was only one feasible thing to do to solve this problem. I had to cancel all our concerts and declare that if I couldn't be Barbara, there would be no more Mandrell sisters. I dramatically jumped off the stage, and that was our very last performance. The patio that I painstakingly hosed down every concert day soon collected leaves and debris, and the red picnic table rotted that summer, unfit to be used as a stage ever again. Ha! I had won.

That was not leadership—it was a dictatorship. If I had been a good leader, I'd have shared the microphone and allowed Marcy and Heather to organize a concert themselves. Yes, I was just a child, so I won't be hard on myself for this failure in leadership. Even in the third grade, Marcy understood that she had what it took to be Barbara. Although she took naturally to the role as my backup singer in the beginning, she began to gain confidence in her own ability, so she protested on behalf of Heather and herself. Speaking up is also a trait of leadership. Heather really didn't care. She chimed in because Marcy empowered her, but the truth was Heather was perfectly content being the backup singer because she didn't want to be bothered with the details that went into organizing a concert. While I lined up the lawn chairs for our faux audience, hung the lights on the patio, made flyers, and handed them out, Heather just wanted to show up and sing. Followers get a bad rap, but a great leader understands how important they are to the mission.

Being bossy is not a bad thing. Clearly, I had the propensity for leading others and was extremely comfortable doing it. However, being bossy doesn't constitute leadership. It is so easy to boss people around and borrow strength from your position. When I was Barbara Mandrell, I was the oldest, most famous sister, so I felt I should be in charge. Leadership is far more than being the boss or the oldest, and it would take me many years to learn this lesson.

Because bossing people around seemed to suit me, it was inevitable that I grew up and became a police officer. Even as a pocket-sized cop with a bouncy ponytail, I felt mighty and had no problem showing up on a scene and taking charge. My inner boss was alive and well. Being a police officer on the street feels like you're the boss because a cop is constantly enforcing laws and telling people what to do. Stop speeding, move along, place your hands behind your back—you get the gist. From the moment we enter the police academy, we learn the importance of "command presence." How you carry yourself determines whether people will listen to you. It's funny how that concept is part of the problem in policing. When cops show up and start slinging power and control, the interaction begins with imbalance. Sure, there are times when a scene has to be commanded and secured, but the majority of the time, a respectful dialogue and humanity are needed more than anything else. But I didn't know that at the beginning of my career. I acted the way I was trained to act. Even as a young cop,

I felt like a "boss," but I didn't know a thing about leadership. I only knew that there were great cops I wanted to work *with* and great supervisors I wanted to work *for.*

When I look back on my years as a young cop in the '90s, I see how my leadership traits evolved by emulating those I respected and vowing never to behave like those I didn't. In the '90s, crime was running rampant nationally and in our city. Street gangs infiltrated our neighborhoods, and it wasn't uncommon to respond to several shootings a night. During these years, law-abiding citizens looked to the cops to stop the bloodshed. It wasn't uncommon for us to attend neighborhood meetings and get yelled at for not having a handle on the violence, but I knew we were doing the best we could. We tried to identify the shooters and get witnesses to come forward, so I got frustrated with the people who were angry with us. We cops were out there doing our best to stop the predators in our community by infiltrating and thwarting their crimes. The first time I chased someone with a gun through backyards was a surreal moment for me. I saw the muzzle flash, and my training officer and I immediately started running toward it. My only thought in the moment was to catch the guy with the gun, but after I got home and lay in bed, replaying the night's events, the magnitude of the danger hit me. I suddenly understood that the people on the sidelines blaming us for crime were directing their anger toward us because they had no other outlet. Some of our citizens started their own neighborhood patrol groups and marched the streets armed with flashlights and reflective vests. They weren't cops, but they were standing shoulder to shoulder with us taking back their neighborhoods. It occurred to me that perhaps those who criticized from the sidelines weren't capable of being in the middle of the action themselves, but it still annoyed me that they were the ones pointing fingers. We all have to determine how we can be a part of the solution. Even those who admit they aren't cut out for the arena can still find ways to be productive from the sidelines.

This same metaphor was just as applicable as I moved up in rank. Those sitting in the cheap seats grew in number but now included members of my own department. The small group of malcontents yell the loudest, but they rarely roll their sleeves up and try to solve a problem. Criticism is a byproduct of leadership, and I had a firm grasp on the fact that I chose this path and got comfortable with the noise from the sidelines, but it took a paradigm shift. I had a revelation one day as a lieutenant when deciding to go against the grain and make an unorthodox change to our process regarding productivity. I was a new lieutenant and had a hypothesis that officers would be more productive when they weren't "forced" to produce. I believed that patrol officers, when allowed to do the thing that was in alignment with their skills and talents, would be happier, and the natural consequence would be greater productivity. I decided to allow officers to focus only on what they wanted to do during their shift. Some really liked to enforce traffic laws, while others enjoyed focusing on gang members to thwart shootings. Some were very prevention minded and liked to drive around the city in the middle of the night and alert residents to things that would make them susceptible to becoming a crime victim like unlocked cars or open garages. The only thing they couldn't choose was to do nothing. They had to go out and work, but they didn't have to abide by the old way of doing business, which was to get credit for tickets and arrests. I had the authority to alter the process currently in place because it was the midnight shift, and I was the highest-ranking officer during those hours. Plus, I didn't bother asking my commander for permission to change things up because I decided to beg for forgiveness if it didn't work. I pitched the idea to the sergeants on my shift, and they weren't all on board. Some felt that every officer should do something of everything. I had made up my mind to change course, and despite some pushback, we implemented the change.

What occurred exceeded my own expectations. I had to attend a bimonthly meeting with the other lieutenants called CompStat to report out our respective shift's production. I couldn't wait for that meeting every two weeks because my shift was crushing it. DUIs increased by 150 percent because we had officers who were passionate about enforcing drunk driving laws in order to save lives. Our tickets increased, our drug arrests increased, our crime prevention notices (CPNs) increased by 300 percent. As it turns out, the officers worked harder because they were allowed to work in their niche of expertise. Everyone kept asking what I was doing differently, and I finally revealed our new process. One commander (my tormenter) was especially vocal in disagreement with my method because he felt it was giving officers too much control. Fortunately, the chief was a "numbers" guy, and he couldn't ignore the positive outcome. After that, I learned to diligently focus on the task or outcome I was trying to achieve and not allow anything to disrupt my conviction—even if the idea was far-fetched.

My second life-altering epiphany came later as a commander when I caught myself asking, "What will *they* think?" before making another change to the traditional way of doing things. I remembered all the pushback I'd incurred in the past in trying to defy the old guard and I found myself revisiting this internal dialogue quite often. What will they think?

It occurred to me that we all suffer from that same self-doubt by constantly wondering what others will think of us if we do something bold or different. We are worried what *they* will think. What will *everyone* think? The best moment of my life came after I finally asked myself, "Who is this *they* that I'm so worried about, and why do I give them so much power?" The answer came from a quote from Brené Brown: "I carry a small sheet of paper in my wallet that has written on it the names of people whose opinions of me matter."

I followed her method and got out a piece of paper and made a list of "theys" in my life whose opinion really matters to me. I call them my "Personal Board of Directors," and they are composed of my family, friends, and mentors with strong values and high expectations of me. I have "theys" in the police department as well, and they are officers I respect, and they represent those who come to work every day and give their best. When I begin to worry or the criticism starts to get to me, I refer to my list, and if I'm doing right by them, the noise falls away.

If there is a time where I know that my "theys" would not be proud, I know that I have to make some changes. I've done a pretty good job of siphoning out the noise by reminding myself of my "theys," but if there is ever a time when I'm struggling with being ridiculed or criticized, I convert the criticism to fuel, so I never run out of energy.

When I make decisions in my organization, I disregard the harsh critics and concentrate on the greater number of police officers in my agency and citizens in my community whose opinions matter. They still question decisions and hold me accountable, but they aren't trying to sabotage or harm. Leaders must make sure they create a space where people can question and respectfully dissent. I'll take advice and input from anyone if I know they have the same interest in making our organization better. I'm fighting for and with them.

Unfortunately, there are always going to be boisterous critics on the sidelines who never offer solutions or roll up their sleeves to help. They may even throw proverbial bricks at you. I can't help but believe that they lack the courage to put themselves out there. If I were afraid of bricks getting thrown at me, I'd never show up to work. And if I took the time to correct the misinformation by critics, I'd never get any work done. The best thing to do is sharpen your reflexes and dodge the bricks, then use them to build a foundation for success. There are plenty of people in the arena who are trying their very best to fight the good fight with honor and integrity. Those are my people. Those are my "theys."

AM I WEIRD?

My people are also the bold ones who don't give a damn what others think of them. I got pretty good at embracing my weirdness and getting comfortable with the fact that I didn't fit into the template of what others expected of a police officer and police leader. As a child, I was given permission to be unapologetically me, and I wanted my kids to develop their own shameless identities and confidence in their uniqueness. I wanted to spare them the heartache of experiencing shame. As I look back, I recognize that while my parents did a good job of setting the foundation for me to be an individual, the pressure to fit in and adapt in my early years at

the police department reprogrammed me. Fortunately, I fought
and overcame conforming, but I didn't want that to happen to
my children, so I tried to build them into secure human beings.

The first time I realized how fragile we are at the hands of
others' ridicule came from my son. One day, Jacob, my five-
year-old kindergartener, got off the bus in front of our house. I
always watched the bus pull up and was accustomed to seeing him
laughing and scurrying toward the front door. One of the happi-
est people I'd ever met, Jacob made everyone around him happy.
Even at that young age, he was making people laugh. So I noticed
immediately as he stepped off the bus that his body language
was different. He was dragging his feet and looking down at the
ground as he walked, which captured my attention immediately,
so I walked outside to meet him. My six-year-old daughter, Bailey,
got off the bus right behind him, and I looked to her for information. She shrugged her shoulders as if to say, "I have no idea what's
wrong with him." He gave me a look that I registered as angry
but on the verge of tears. I opened the front door silently, and he
stomped past me, dumped his backpack on the kitchen floor, and
plopped down next to it with his arms crossed. I sat down next to
him, looking at his sullen face, and asked what happened.

He was silent for several moments and then asked, "Mommy,
am I weird?" He had a small speech impediment, so the word
sounded like "wee-rud." My initial reaction was relief because
I was not expecting him to say that, and then I felt the urge to
laugh because he sounded adorable, but his face was so stoic that
I successfully concealed my grin. I suddenly understood this was
a crisis of magnitude from a five-year-old perspective. He continued, "A boy in my class called me weird." I paused so I could

formulate my response. Bailey froze in place, and she was watching me carefully to see what I would say. It was apparent that Jacob was looking for reassurance that he was not, in fact, weird.

As a mother, I had the credibility to invalidate what his classmate had said, and I could have done it swiftly so that Jacob could move on to his Legos, Play-Doh, and other things that occupied his five-year-old existence. I could simply tell him that he was not weird. The problem was that I would have been lying because Jacob was very weird. And weird was a bit of an understatement. He refused to wear his polo shirt correctly, so every morning, he would come downstairs with it on backward with the collar hiding his mouth. He chewed the backward collars of his shirts, so I had to replace them often. He wore a knit cap that he refused to take off his head. When I say refused, I'm not kidding. He went through this phase for about nine months, and I had to wait until he fell asleep to stealthily remove it from his head to wash it. In every picture taken of Jacob in 2005, that stupid hat is on his head. He would randomly burst out in song in the most inopportune times, and he was annoyingly loud about it. All of these things my weirdo kid did flashed in my mind.

So I took a deep breath and answered, "Yes. You are very weird!" A look of confusion came over his face, and I could almost see his cogs turning. A boy had called him weird. It was clearly not meant to be a compliment. And I, his own mother, did not discount the notion. I could have, but I didn't. The problem was his classmate was right: Jacob was the weirdest kid I knew. Both of my kids were weird. It was their weirdness that made—makes—them funny, unpredictable, and wonderful. I continued, "And so am I! So is Bailey. It's one of the best parts about us!" When I explained to Jacob that being weird was the very thing that made him inter-esting, his face softened. I told him that I had spent a lot of time trying to hide my weirdness, and I had realized that being weird was far more interesting than being dull.

"Yes! You are weird!" I declared. *"Fly your freaky flag!"* Both of my children repeated the mantra while bouncing around the kitchen. "Fly your freaky flag!" Jacob said he was going to go to school and tell that kid he was right—he is weird. I had some reservations about how that was going to go, but it didn't really matter in the big scheme of things because Jacob's paradigm had shifted so much that he could not be deterred by the bully at school. It was Oliver Wendell Holmes who said, "Man's mind, once stretched by a new idea, never regains its original dimensions." For Jacob, there was no going back to ordinary.

I didn't realize how that small exchange with my son was a monumental lesson in my children's lives. A few months later, I volunteered to read to my daughter's first grade class. I walked to Bailey's desk and saw a Post-it note that was taped on all four sides and affixed to the corner of her desk. In her own handwrit-ing was written "Fly your freaky flag." I knew at that moment that I didn't want them to do what I did. I didn't want them to ever stop being perfectly themselves to fit in. I understood that I needed to remind them incessantly of this lesson, so their foun-dations weren't as shaky as mine had been. It was a lesson that I wish wasn't so remedial for me throughout my life. As long as you aren't hurting anyone and you are doing the right thing for the right reasons, be you. And when someone calls you weird, smile and unapologetically say, "Yes, I am."

WHY NOT YOU?

Despite my having learned to embrace my weirdness, the little voice in my head is often worse than the noise from the sidelines. When I was a lieutenant interviewing for the commander position (second in command) in my police department, I psyched myself out, reminding myself why I probably wouldn't get the job. I was younger than my colleagues and had only been at the lieutenant's rank for two years. Maybe it was true that I needed to be in SWAT gear to be taken seriously. Did I really think I had a shot at this position? The inner voice was worse than the outside noise because my inner voice was privy to all my insecurities. Whenever this happens to me, I usually snap out of it, but sometimes, my insecure inner self delivers persistent and sabotaging messages. That little naysayer can brainwash you if you aren't careful, and you might begin to believe the bullshit you tell yourself about not being good enough. That voice is powerful and influential, and you believe everything you think, so *change the way you think*. I often must call on my inner bossy girl to take over. Instead of comparing myself to others, I focus on the skills and talents that have brought me this far. It's amazing how your mindset shifts when you change your thoughts.

I changed the narrative in my head from "Why me?" to "Wait a hot second! Why *not* me?" Seriously, why *not* me? I had earned a master's degree and graduated from the FBI National Academy, along with many other prestigious law enforcement programs. I had proven myself a loyal and competent officer, sergeant, and lieutenant, and I knew I would be good as a commander. My self-doubt crept in again when I was announced a finalist for the Chicago police superintendent's position. My inner voice told me

I had no business applying to lead the second-largest police force in the nation—especially because my agency was so much smaller. And then I realized how preposterous that talk was. Whether a person leads a team of thirty, three hundred, or thirteen thousand, the same leadership principles apply, albeit on a different scale. Leadership is leadership. Since becoming a commander, I had added another master's degree in security studies from the Naval Postgraduate School, and I led the second-largest police department in my state. Formal education aside, my strengths lie in building trust with our residents and reducing crime in communities by drawing on the talents of our officers. I was born to do this. I've got this.

You will have critics, and people will judge you, but if you are right with your "theys," you can tune out the noise from the outside world. I'm not saying it's easy, but by practicing it consciously and habitually, confidence will become a virtue you possess. The next time you are faced with a challenge or are pondering whether to pursue something in your life, ask yourself, "What is the worst thing that could happen?" Maybe the answer is that people will judge or criticize you. Maybe it's bigger than that. But once you have determined what it is, you can decide if you are willing to accept it. Make peace with it. Then do it.

CHAPTER ELEVEN

THE PATH OF NO REGRET

I met Matt in 1991 when we both started as police cadets. I was seventeen years old, and he was eighteen. We married in 1996, and our entire lives revolved around our jobs. We socialized with cops on our days off, and everything was cop centric. I loved everything about being a cop. When I worked in patrol, I was often told by my supervisors that I spent too much time on my calls trying to solve problems instead of taking the reports and moving onto the next call. My curious spirit pushed me to solve the puzzle presented in each call from dispatch. If it was a neighbor dispute, I wanted to mediate. If it was a domestic violence call, I wanted to determine the factors that led to the violence. Most cops just wanted to take down the basic information and get out or quickly make an arrest. I don't know why I thought so differently, but I did. Looking back, it might have had something to do with my own childhood. Maybe I thought I needed to fix everyone else's crises since I didn't have control of my own growing up. I didn't care about arrest numbers or tickets, but at the time in my department, the emphasis was on quantity versus quality, so I produced just enough to keep my sergeant happy.

I was happier when I could engage a social service agency to assist with an offender because I learned very quickly that arresting people didn't always solve the underlying issue. That philosophy landed me a job in the Community Oriented Policing unit, where I loved to work. We weren't tied to the radio to answer 9-1-1 calls, and my primary function was to talk to the residents of my assigned district, assess their problems, and develop a response. We had total autonomy, conducting overt and covert operations to combat violent crime and resolve quality-of-life issues. In attending neighborhood meetings and connecting with the residents, I found my niche. As an outgoing officer, I liked to talk to people and figure out how I could fix their problems.

While busy living the dream in my job, a lieutenant tapped me for a team charged with researching and building a new unit within the department to investigate domestic violence cases. I wasn't interested at first. I was so happy in the Community Policing unit, yet I understood why I had been a natural choice for the lieutenant, who appreciated my knack for determining the root causes of violence in domestic calls. I loved the challenge of determining the origin of the conflict, and I was often chastised by my fellow cops for putting so much energy into the calls. The cops who had been doing this a long time told me these family issues were complex and said it was idealistic to think I could solve a problem in twenty minutes that has probably taken twenty years to develop. I knew they were right, but I still had a burning need to understand how things could break so badly that the police had to be called. I knew from my own upbringing that substance abuse was an aggravating factor, and because I wasn't a stranger to dysfunction, I felt oddly comfortable policing these situations. Coming from a tumultuous childhood helped me understand those in crisis and made me better at my job. I identified with the people and the problems that I was called upon to police, and domestics were my forte. Eventually, I left community policing and helped to build the Domestic Violence Reduction Unit from the ground up, and I spent nearly five years as a detective in that unit. We began to understand the consequences of kids' growing up in violent homes—they would be doomed to repeat the cycle without intervention—so we partnered with a domestic violence shelter and started teaching conflict resolution to kids as early as kindergarten. I learned so much about the psychology of human behavior while working in that unit. I discovered that it's easy for everyone on the outside looking in to say, "Why don't you leave him?" and then cast judgment. I uttered that question myself until I started talking with victims of domestic abuse in order to understand. I learned that physical abuse rarely occurs early in the relationship. Instead, it often begins with imposing control in seemingly insignificant ways. One victim said her boyfriend told her he didn't want her to hang out with her friends as much because he wanted to be with her. She initially thought that was sweet but didn't realize that she was slowly phasing out her friends. Then he said he would handle all the finances. This seemed like a positive move in their relationship and one less thing she would have to worry about. Then he started to with-hold money and chastise her spending. Then the verbal abuse started, and she endured insults that chipped away at her self-esteem. The first physical act came when he shoved her. Then he blocked the door so she couldn't leave. Soon after, a fist flew into her eye. After a few years, she realized she was a battered woman and was alone without friends or resources. There were so many similar stories, and I developed a deep passion and commitment to assisting victims. But I also learned that no matter how hard we tried, many victims went back to their abusers. We had plenty of success stories, but I found myself becoming disillusioned with my job because I felt like a failure when a victim returned to an abusive relationship.

I also started to realize something about myself by watching my partner, Doug. He seemed to have an infinite amount of patience for victims who opted to return to their abusers, no matter how much work we did to get them to a safe place where they could start over. I understood why a person stays in an abusive relationship and even became a trainer to teach other police officers everything I learned about the cycle of violence and to understand how domestic violence doesn't begin on the first date with a punch to the face. I taught them the evolution of abuse with the goal of getting them to police these situations with compassion. In trying to teach compassion to others, I began to realize that I was not practicing what I was teaching. I started to feel impatient and become irritable with the domestic violence victims who refused to help themselves. I started to feel angry at the abusers who refused to quit drinking or doing drugs even though they knew it hurt their children. I wondered how some people could put their kids through the trauma of terror when it came to physical and substance abuse, realizing that my anger was misdirected because I had never faced my own demons. I learned that you can never escape your past because my own life experiences began to creep in. Until my work in the domestic violence unit, I was able to put my childhood trauma from my dad's alcohol abuse in a proverbial box and stow it away in my subconsciousness. No matter how much we believe we can avoid pain by ignoring it or pushing it away, it will eventually find a way to escape and confront us. Pain and suffering will always prevail over avoidance. Some good came from my past infiltrating my present. Gaining an understanding of why victims wouldn't leave their harmful relationships made me understand my mom a little better, and in the cases I worked, I often got a pang of familiarity as a memory would come bubbling to the surface. This started to happen more and more frequently, and all the things I'd suppressed as a child came crashing forcefully into consciousness. By this time, I had given birth to my second child and was very close with my mom, who helped babysit as Matt and I juggled different shifts. Age and experience offered me a different perspective of my mom, and it became clear to me that she did the very best she could with what she had. She was an amazing grandmother, and there wasn't a day that went by when she didn't show up for me and the kids.

Despite the revelation that my mom was a victim of being in love with a raging alcoholic, I still was struggling with the bubbling up of my past, and it forced me to confront memories that I thought I had successfully stifled. I was sixteen when my mom and dad divorced, and around that same time, my dad resigned from the police department (not by his own choice) and moved semipermanently onto a barstool. His being a cop had been the thing I admired most about him, so when he wasn't one anymore, I felt as though my superhero had left. I spent my childhood embarrassed of him when he was drunk but worshipping him when he was in uniform. When I applied to be a police cadet in high school, the sergeant that interviewed me had worked with my dad, and I secretly wondered if being my father's daughter would keep me from getting hired. I decided to confront it head-on in my interview by declaring that I had no knowledge of whatever caused my dad to resign from the police department, and assuming it wasn't good, I asked that they still hire me on my own merit. The sergeant pulled me aside after the interview and said something like "Your dad got the shaft and was the scapegoat for a captain and a lieutenant." I didn't have a clue what he was talking about, but I was so relieved that they decided to hire me.

I didn't see my dad much during my high school years, but when I started working at the police department, we started talking more. Now we had something in common as I worked for the same people he knew, so it was fun to bounce things off him and share my stories. I knew he was genuinely happy for me because I loved my job so much. He would tell me whom to avoid at the police department and whom I could go to for guidance. He was always right. I loved him and tried to maintain a relationship with him because, despite his barstool lifestyle, he never stopped making me think deeply about things, and he still made me laugh. We had a ritual of meeting for breakfast once a month, which continued after my children, Bailey and Jacob, were born but only during his short window of sobriety early in the morning. I wanted my kids to know their grandpa and learn his story of migrating from Norway and all the other great things he had taught me. That all changed one morning when I loaded Bailey in her car seat and Jacob in his infant carrier and trekked off to meet him. I sat for an hour waiting in the restaurant with the kids, but he never showed up. It stirred up memories of all the times he had forgotten to pick me up in my childhood, so I decided then that I would not put my own children through the same disappointment I had felt when he didn't show up or broke a solemn vow that he would not drink before one of my school events.

The parallels of the cases I worked in the domestic violence unit and my own childhood started to bother me, and I felt all the old emotions rising to the surface. The longer I stayed in that assignment, the more I realized that I had to look in the mirror and admit that I had become ineffective because I hadn't learned how to make peace with my past. I became impatient with victims who didn't leave their abusers, and I started to develop a feeling of apathy. I went to my lieutenant and told him our childcare provider wasn't working out and asked to be transferred to the swing shift, so I could be with my kids during the day. That was true(ish). Moving to the afternoon shift solved my childcare problems and got me out of the unit, but I didn't want to admit that I had been struggling with my assignment. I was granted a request to leave the unit and return to patrol, where I became a field training officer for new recruits and signed up to take the promotional test to sergeant. I succeeded in outrunning the demons. For a while.

THE PATH REVEALS ITSELF

After I got back on the street, I kept busy enough to distract myself from the fact that my marriage was unraveling. I know I shortchanged the recruits assigned to me while being consumed with my personal baggage. This time on patrol taught me a lesson that has served me well in leadership positions: it's impossible to leave your home life at home, and it's impossible to leave your work life at work. Our personal and professional lives are made up of moments, and just because one moment happens at work doesn't mean we don't carry it with us when we cross the threshold of our homes. Conversely, our intimate relationships consume us, and it is absurd to think that they don't affect how we perform in our other roles. Looking back on that time in my life, I know now that I should have sought help. But I didn't want anyone to know what was happening in my marriage. We were a picture-perfect couple from the outside, and I didn't want that image to become distorted. I grew up feeling ashamed and embarrassed of being raised in a bar and everything that went with it, so being married to Matt allowed me to escape that shame. I got used to being a part of the picture-perfect Ziman family, and I craved the image so much that I didn't want to admit what was happening.

By this time, having roughly nine years on the job and having ascended the sergeant's list, I was promoted and assigned to the 3:00 p.m.–11:00 p.m. shift. Matt and I had been married for seven years by then, so he was working midnights, and we never saw each other. We were just kids when we met, and the truth was, we were never really compatible. Matt is a very traditional man, perfectly content with a small circle and a steady, consistent lifestyle. I see now that it was this quality that I gravitated toward when I was seventeen years old. He and his family felt safe to me because I was running from chaos and uncertainty. But as we navigated our twenties as cops and young parents, our differences became glaring. He was an introvert while I was an extrovert. He liked sci-fi while I liked everything but. In retrospect, I had more in common with his parents and sister than with him. His dad was also a cop, an ambitious and academic one to boot, and we talked about books and getting degrees. I spent more time with his sister and his mom—some of my most favorite people—since Matt worked the night shift. But a good relationship with my husband's family couldn't save the marriage of two good people who simply weren't right for one another.

When we got divorced, I felt divorced from the entire family, which was devastating to me. I spent many years consumed with guilt, but that feeling dissipated over the years because time and distance are miraculous healers. What's more, our kids are now in their twenties and seem to be well-adjusted humans who contribute positively to mankind (but I'll be following them closely into adulthood to continue my assessment). Through it all, Matt and I did what a lot of parents find challenging to do: we got along and didn't fight over the kids. I promised myself that I would never say a disparaging word about him to my kids because policing has given me a front-row seat into how parents use children as pawns in broken relationships. Like all my lessons, I learned what not to do by witnessing terrible parents in the course of my job. I had the clarity to understand that they are half his blood, and to say anything hurtful about him would be insulting to them. To this day, Matt is the same person for me that he has always been. Even when I remarried, he remained always present and always steadfast.

CHAPTER TWELVE

WILL YOUR REAL IDENTITY PLEASE STAND UP?

I thought I would make a great wife when I got married, but that didn't turn out to be the case. I convinced myself that since I wasn't good at marriage, I would try to be really good at my job. As a new sergeant, I emerged with the grand idea that I would be the best sergeant the officers assigned to me ever had. I wanted to be different from the crotchety supervisors who disappeared during the shift and got annoyed if you bothered them. The bad bosses didn't care about their people and seemed to be checked out. The goal for them was never to be called upon, and the cops learned how to navigate around them. It was extremely danger-ous to bother them while they were eating, so I set out to do the exact opposite and proudly proclaimed myself a servant leader. It worked. My squad was performing, and I was so excited to be in a leadership position. I loved coming to work every day, and I tried to set the example of being cheerful and energetic. Once again, I had found my stride, and in those moments, I felt as though I was flourishing because I was being authentically me. When I tried to be someone I wasn't in both my marriage and my job, I felt discombobulated, but at this moment, all was right with the world.

And then I accidentally fell in love. I didn't mean to fall in love, and I certainly didn't mean to fall in love with a woman. In my early thirties, I was a mess because my friend Christine was now more than a friend, which was confusing and terrifying and wonderful all at the same time. I knew of Christine (a.k.a. Chris) several years before I actually met her. She was a new officer working midnights with Matt, so he mentioned her all the time, so much so that I got snippy (a.k.a. jealous) about it. Matt forgot his phone one night when he went to work, and out of a sound sleep I awoke to his phone ringing in the middle of the night. Following the sound to his closet and flipping the phone open (yes, it was a flip phone) to see her name on the screen, without thinking, I called the number back. When she answered, I hung up. I felt like a middle school psycho.

When he got home in the morning after his shift, I think I said something snarky like "Your girlfriend was calling you in the middle of the night." His dismissive laugh chapped my ass even more, which caused me to go deeper into a psychotic rant. When I finished, he looked at me with a face that I interpreted as "Are you done?" and replied, "She has a girlfriend."

Boy did I feel stupid.

I also felt guilty for hating her before I knew her—especially since I had jumped to the wrong conclusion. Several weeks later, I was at the city garage gassing up my squad when she pulled up. We struck up a conversation, and I was really nice to her in my attempt to make up for hating her (even though she didn't know I hated her). She mentioned something about how awesome Matt is and then said we should grab drinks one night. On the 3:00 p.m.– 11:00 p.m. shift, I didn't socialize much because I had to race home to relieve my mom, who watched the kids between the time Matt left for work and I got home. One night, I asked my mom to stay a little longer so I could meet Chris for a drink at the bar where her girlfriend worked. I went out of guilt but also because I really missed going out and being social. That night, Chris and I talked for hours, and I felt as though I had known her all my life. Her girlfriend was nice, and I found out much later that she told Chris that night I would be the end of them.

I didn't see it coming. Chris and I became great friends, and she turned into my best friend. She was previously married to a man and had two kids with him. After they divorced, she met her girlfriend, and I was intrigued by her story. We became inseparable, but I wasn't gay. It was during this time that Matt and I were unraveling, and she was there. The unraveling and the entanglement were messy, and I was disoriented.

I'm not a lesbian. But I'm also not *not* a lesbian. I had never been with a woman, but because I was having feelings for a woman, I started connecting some dots backward to understand myself, and suddenly things made sense to me. In third grade, I loved my teacher. Miss Smith was amazing and kind to me. This is not unusual for a young girl to love her teacher, but something unusual did happen. One day, Miss Smith told the class she had an announcement to share, a man walked into our classroom, and she said they were getting married. All the girls swooned, clapped, and ran to hug her. I sat in my seat pissed off. I crossed my arms and glared at her soon-to-be husband and never got over it. I had an amazing boyfriend in high school and dated a few guys before Matt and I got together, but as I looked back, I realized I had never been boy crazy like my girlfriends, and I had never heard a romantic poem or a love song and felt anything I could relate to.

Even at the beginning of my relationship with Matt, I remember missing my female friends and feeling as though the connection I had with them was deeper than what I had with Matt. I chalked it up to being emotionally unavailable on account of my childhood and my parents' failed marriage. Plus, most straight women I've talked with say they have deep connections with their female friends that are on a different level than with their husbands. So I just assumed my deeper connection with women was normal. I'm not even sure what normal means because being "connected" to another human is as natural and normal as it gets. It would have been more obvious to me if it was a sexual connection, but that wasn't the case. I loved Matt when I married him, but I now understand that I didn't have a clue who I was at age seventeen when I met him or even at age twenty-three when we got married. I don't think you really know who you are until you get out of your twenties. I felt like a full-on adult in my twenties, but now that I'm in my fourth decade, I realize how absurd that was. My twenties were the decade when I broke away from my childhood beliefs and the people who sculpted them. It was the first time of my life that I was truly free to think and feel independently of what I had been taught. My twenties were a time of self-discovery spent figuring out who I actually was and not what someone had told me to be.

I tried to unfall in love with Chris. I didn't want to be a lesbian. I didn't want the label attached to me, so I spent years fighting it and pushing her away. I tried to wish it away, but that's not how these things work. We tried to go our separate ways a million times because she was convinced that I wouldn't settle down with her if I didn't have a chance to be single first. She worried that if I went from my marriage to her, I would begin to resent never having been on my own. And she knew I was grappling with my sexuality, so she proposed I break away from her to date other people and figure it out. That sounds ludicrous, I know, but she was willing to let me go figure it out to be sure I wanted to be with her. That's the most unselfish kind of love I've ever known. And she was right. I hadn't been single since I was seventeen, and now at thirty, I was trying to figure out who I was. This would go on for years until I finally reconciled my inner conundrum and stopped fighting both who I was and the fact that the universe wouldn't allow me to let her go. I found my way back to her, and the only reason she is still by my side is because she refused to give up on me.

I fell in love with Chris for all these reasons. She is fiercely loyal in a way that I don't understand. When someone harms me, I am quick to cut ties because I don't like feeling vulnerable. If you hurt me, I walk away and won't look back. I don't have the time or energy to devote to people who bring negative energy into my life. It's part of the reason I am good at my job: despite my outward femininity, I am not ruled by emotion at all. Chris is emotional and forgiving, and she stays with people. I want to be more like her.

I spent my adult life believing I was broken because I came

from dysfunction. Despite my dad being an alcoholic, I identified with him and thought I was wired like him. I believed I was incapable of loving and committing to someone. I always had one foot out the door and an "I don't need anyone" attitude. My kids were the only thing that mattered, and I was convinced I'd be fine otherwise. The thought of needing someone made me feel weak. I'm sure this emotional deficit came from watching my mom's heart break over and over. I remember vowing never to need another human being. I'd figure it out myself.

I never came out as gay to anyone. I refused partly because I was still grappling with the idea, and I didn't consider myself a lesbian. I was defiant about having a label affixed to me. When Chris and her kids moved in with Bailey, Jacob, and me, I didn't make a declaration to anyone. I decided to take Chris with me for one of my breakfast dates with my dad shortly after we moved in together, and I introduced her with no explanation. After I returned home from breakfast, I received an email from my dad in all caps: I REALLY LIKE CHRIS AND I AM HAPPY FOR YOU. My mom did something similar, only it was far more verbose. She penned an email telling me that since being with Chris, I was more myself than I had ever been. It went on for pages, and she called out our relationship, saying she loved us. I panicked and deleted it. I had the opposite problem that most have when "coming out." I had people trying to drag me "out" by showering me with love and acceptance, but I was the asshole who wouldn't allow it. I was trying to stay hidden in the proverbial closet.

I don't know why I fought it so hard. I think I had an idea of what I was supposed to do and who I was supposed to be, and being in a same-sex relationship didn't fit the template I had for myself. I had it figured out in my professional life because I got to a point where I didn't care what anyone thought as long as I was doing my best for the police department. But I imposed a different set of rules on myself for my personal life, and that is where the concept of the "theys" in my life was fully realized. I learned that it applied to *all* parts of my life. I spent my formative years being judged at my private school and felt shame about being a baby barfly. I finally shed the shame and was proud of who I had become, yet being gay felt like I was inviting shame back into my life by worrying what people would think. This is the remedial lesson I have had to learn over and over until it finally stuck. Human beings aren't meant to compartmentalize their lives. We are meant to be our authentic selves, and stifling who we are meant to be is harmful to the soul. I still don't subscribe to labels, but I now know that shame is debilitating and heavy, and courage is the only remedy.

I'll never forget the advice given to me by a close family friend in 2007. He told me his story of coming to terms with realizing he was gay and the residual pain in breaking off his engagement to a woman. But the real lesson he taught me was about shame. At the time, he was a relatively new doctor specializing in pediatrics, and he got to know the families of his patients pretty well. When meeting new patients, he said the organic unfolding of conversation typically began with seemingly innocuous questions like "Are you married?" or "Do you have a family?" Most people don't think twice about this natural sharing of information, unless they are hiding something. In my own life, I found myself tiptoeing around pronouns when someone asked if I was in a relationship and did everything I could to avoid fully disclosing that I had a female partner. He decided not to tiptoe, so when someone asked if he was married, his response was bold and matter of fact: "Yes, and my husband's name is Ryan." He said the awkward moment that typically transpired was almost always followed by a positive response. I understood what he was trying to teach me. If he were to dance around or avoid his truth, he would be allowing shame to occupy the space, and it would give permission for others to do the same. By confronting it confidently, he thwarted others' outward judgment, but if they judged him, he didn't care. I began applying his lesson to my own life. I'm a woman in a same-sex relationship, but I can hide it if I choose, meaning that when people meet me, they automatically assume I'm married to a man. When people ask, "What does your husband do?" my answer is, "My wife is a child sex abuse detective." Each time I watch the same reaction that my friend described, and ninety-nine out of one hundred times, people are awesome about it. Shame is heavy, so when we feel embarrassed about who we are, we send that signal to others. I admit that it was hard for me at the beginning, but once I got used to it, I grew into being confident about who I am. Own your truth unapologetically no matter what it is. And if by chance someone isn't accepting, you are better off finding out right away. You don't want anyone in your space who simply tolerates you. Let those people move on and out of your life. Addition by subtraction.

When Chris and I got together, I gained two bonus children in Megan and Jimmy, and our blended family has been full of ups and downs just like every family. Four kids blended together under one roof makes life loud. As an only child, I wasn't used to sibling rivalry, so every time our boys started physically fighting, I thought something was wrong with them. The boys were five and eight when we moved in together, and they fought like they were in the WWF. I started taking a poll at work and felt better when everyone assured me that it was normal. People were happy to show me scars on their bodies inflicted by their siblings and added that they liked each other as adults. I felt better and stopped trying to force everyone into anger management therapy.

Our blended family is my happy place. Now that they are grown, I realize what a gift I was given in meeting Chris and how my life unfolded as it was meant to. She has been such a constant in my life, and she is the reason for the successes in my career. I would never have achieved what I have without her. She makes me feel bulletproof.

CHAPTER THIRTEEN

COPY THE ANGELS

Over the years, I started meeting my dad for breakfast again because Chris made me. As I said, I write people off and don't look back. Chris convinced me not to do that to my dad, so she forced me to reinstate our breakfast dates. Sometimes I took the kids, but most of the time it was Chris and I who met him monthly at his favorite diner. My mom still maintained a life-insurance policy on him, so every few months, she would ask me how my dad was doing. It took me a while to figure out she was asking whether he had one foot in the grave, so she could collect. "How's your dad's health?" she would ask. My dad thought it was hilarious and told me to pass along that he wasn't going to die before her out of sheer stubbornness.

I met my dad for the last time right before his seventieth birthday at the diner in 2015. He sat down and ordered his usual strawberry crepes and waited a few moments before he removed a baseball hat from his coat pocket and placed it on his head. It was a hat that had a date embroidered on it—the date President Obama was slated to leave office. He was an ultraconservative, had no use for a Democratic president, and got a kick out of being openly obstinate about it. He knew I loved Barack Obama, so this purchase was solely to mess with me. He giggled as I finally computed what the date meant, and when I started laughing and shaking my head, he smugly wore an expression of satisfaction. He had this weird thing he did when he was making fun of me. He simultaneously laughed and said, "Tee hee," his sign that he had achieved a good ribbing at my expense. I have never known anyone else in my life to sound out laughy words, and it was hilarious.

Once he was satisfied with my reaction to his hat, I started in on my monthly lecture about taking better care of himself by eating better and cutting down on his drinking. He had some health issues but nothing too serious, so he politely listened, not really hearing me because he was going to do what he damn well pleased. He had a hip replacement a year earlier, and his doc said the other hip would soon need replacing, but the first surgery sucked so bad that he refused to do the second. I know the reason he didn't want the surgery was because it was too painful for him to dry out in the hospital. When I was slated to pick him up from the rehab facility a few weeks after his surgery, he begged me to stop and get him a case of beer. I refused. Chris ended up buying it for him, which I pouted about. So he endured the residual pain from his bad hip, but his case of beer a day tempered it. I'm sure sitting on a bar stool day in and day out wasn't great for a bad hip, but he didn't care. He said, "I would rather die happy than give up what I love." Fair enough, I suppose. Besides, I genuinely thought this guy was immortal. We joked that the alcohol had pickled his organs, so he was never going to die.

Over breakfast, we talked about my interview for the chief's job coming up in the next few weeks. He knew that four candidates were competing for the position and that one had been a tormentor of mine. Before we parted ways after breakfast in the parking lot, my dad told me, "Give 'em hell in the interview." Then he said, "Illegitimi non carborundum." I knew the phrase well. He had uttered it to me many times over the years when I told him about some of my challenges at work with my saboteurs. "Don't let the bastards get you down." I smiled and walked away.

My dad passed away several days before my interview with the mayor for the chief's job. It feels misleading to say he passed away because that suggests a serene ending to his life. It's not the same in my mind, knowing he had killed himself.

I was in my office when I received a call from one of our police officers, Nikole Peterson. With a tone of hesitation, she said she had received a phone call from a friend of hers who bartended at the VFW that my dad frequented daily. This friend told her that my dad hadn't been to the bar in a few days and that she was worried about him. The moment those words came out of Nikole's mouth, I knew my dad was dead. He went to the bar every single day, and the only time he didn't was when he was hospitalized. I told Nikole I would head that way, and she said she would as well. I called Chris and told her I was pretty sure Hans was dead. All I remember is her telling me not to move. She picked me up from the police department, and we drove to my dad's house in the next town over. And by house, I mean garage. My dad lived in a garage that he rented from his friend because that's where you live when you spend all your money on alcohol.

When we pulled up, Nikole was walking toward me from the garage and her face told me what I already knew. The only medical issue he had was a distended bowel, and the remedy was surgery. He refused to have the surgery because there was a risk that he might need a colostomy bag, and that was not an option for him. He was too proud and said he'd rather die. So that's what I assumed happened: his bowel had exploded because he was too stubborn to get a simple procedure. Chris walked into my dad's garage apartment and quickly came back out and wouldn't let me enter. She said he was on the floor by his bed. I was pacing up and down the driveway in disbelief that he was dead. The police officers from that jurisdiction arrived on the scene and went into my dad's garage. They were in there much longer, and when they came out, one of them said, "Did you all not see the gun under his chin? He shot himself in the head."

Plot twist.

How did Chris and Nikole miss the gun and the bullet wound? In their defense, Nikole went in and out as quickly as Chris did, and they didn't look too closely. This was also because he was buck naked. As an aside, my dad was a cop. And cops know that people will eventually find the person who committed suicide, so it would stand to reason that if you're going to kill yourself, you should put on pants. Tee hee.

I have always hated responding to suicide scenes. I find them to be so challenging because those who find the victims are often the ones who loved them the most. I have never understood how a person could be so selfish as to leave one's family with that final memory and, especially in the cases with no note or warning, leave them wondering why.

The anger I have felt on behalf of family members has been real. And now *I'm* that family member trying to get inside the head of a man who chose to leave this world without saying goodbye to his one and only child. I made Chris go back into the garage apartment and get the suicide note. It was hard for her to tell me he didn't leave one. I told her to check his computer because there was no way he left without writing something to me in all caps. I vacillated between profound sadness and wanting to beat my fists against his chest. What we did find in his garage house was every article ever written about me in the newspaper. He kept everything that mentioned me along with photographs taken over the years. I know he loved me, and I know how proud he was. But I can't seem to get over his not saying goodbye.

And then I thought about the man who was my father and the demons he fought throughout his life. He was two people to me, so I mastered the art of compartmentalizing both. I was flooded with memories of sitting on his lap watching television shows like Jacques Cousteau's underwater exploration and Carl Sagan's personal voyage through the cosmos. I flashed back to his reading me excerpts from psychologist Carl Jung, and I was bored by it but I pretended to love it because he did. He also exposed me to *The Benny Hill Show*, and I loved listening to his thunderous cackle even though I didn't understand what was so funny. He took things apart and put them back together, and his degree from the DeVry Institute of Technology resulted in our garage being turned into a television repair shop. He was a police officer by trade but a technical hobbyist during his off hours. I sat in his workshop with him, and he let me melt spools of metal using the soldering gun (another example of perilous parenting in hindsight). I didn't realize until adulthood how much his curiosity about life was woven through the tapestry of mine and how it has manifested into my insatiable thirst for knowledge. He's the reason I became a police officer, and I'm blessed that his military and law enforcement service was instilled in me.

Then there was the other side of my father. I would often sneak into his liquor cabinet and pour bottle after bottle down the drain, so he would stop drinking. His restless mind was likely the result of his addictive personality (or maybe vice versa), and I'm not sure he was ever able to quiet his thoughts—so he drank them away. I wrote him letters as a child and begged him to stop drinking. He never acknowledged me and continued to replace every bottle I washed away in the sink. Every night when he came home from the bar, I learned to tailor my behavior to his mood. I learned the skillful art of adaptation as a result.

The demons of addiction took over his life, and they wrote his script and downward spiral. He lost everything that was important to him, but in my mind, it was his choice. My dad is the reason I thought everyone who enjoyed a cocktail in their own home was an alcoholic. It wasn't until I was in my thirties that I finally understood moderation and balance were the key to everything in life, but I still find myself triggered by those who indulge to excess regularly. It's part of the reason I grapple with understanding addiction—because I have spent my entire life convinced it's a choice. Those who are alcoholics and addicts choose their poison over their loved ones. At least that's what I used to believe.

He was seventy years old when he decided he didn't want to

be here anymore. He chose to leave this life using the weapon he carried on his side as a police officer. And now I'm left with remnants of his dual existence, trying to make sense of it all by separating the darkness from the light. Our parents and other influencers are fallible and imperfect, and the way to peace is to recognize and embrace both their light and dark. I choose to cling to the angel memory of a man whose energy is making its way to Carl Sagan's vast cosmos, and I'm going to let go of the man with the demons.

When he died, I had to confront my own demons and then let them go with him. Even though I was so much of him, I wasn't all of him. I stopped living as though I was ready to run and found peace where I stood. I realized that we are all a juxtaposition of good intentions and bad actions. Every single one of us is damaged and fallible and perfect and pristine. We must copy the angels and learn from the demons.

CHAPTER FOURTEEN

LABELS ARE FOR SOUP

After my dad killed himself, I was convinced he landed south of heaven. His death made me revisit my tumultuous relationship with my own faith once again. This was a pattern for me. After I left my Christian school, I stopped going to church because I needed a break from organized religion. The curriculum was so Bible-centric that I wanted to see what life was like outside the Bible bubble. Then, I had a bit of a spiritual crisis in high school and followed my never-wavering Christian mom to her church. I was trying to find a line to Jesus again, thinking that I might need some direction.

Later in life, I would once again find myself searching for Jesus, but this time it was because I felt my children needed exposure to religion, so they could decide for themselves what they believed. My mom and dad had provided me with the unintended gift of conversation surrounding religion. My parents never fought about it, but my mom often expressed frustration at my dad poking fun at her deep-seated beliefs. I don't recall it being mean-spirited, but when my dad called my mom's religion a cult, she became unglued. I certainly understood that my family had adopted diverse belief systems, so I wanted my children to learn about different religions on their own and choose for themselves. Despite being detached from religion as a parent, I still felt a strong tether to spirituality and wanted that for my children. But I had failed to expose them to any religion. By this time, I was in a new relationship—with a woman. All the teachings and scripture about homosexuality being a sin started bubbling inside me; I needed to find Jesus to explain that I had never planned for this to happen and hopefully get him to understand it wasn't my fault. God is a forgiving God, so I needed to be forgiven and get my kids' souls right with the Lord. I couldn't shake the fire-and-brimstone lessons of my elementary years at Aurora Christian.

Chris and I started church shopping. Between us, we had four children who needed inoculating, but it was tricky to find a church that was welcoming to same-sex couples. We opted for one of those progressive megachurches that had a full-on band. We jammed to Christian rock, which was fine. But it didn't feed my soul or intellect. Then, we opted for one of those tiny unitarian churches with a rainbow flag on the door. I decided that this would be our home. They were accepting and liberal, and I knew in my heart this was the place I'd been searching for my entire life. I was wrong. The sermon was political and very liberal, and I didn't connect to the message. Just as at the megachurch, I didn't fit in. Everything smelled like patchouli, and people wore tie-dye—I don't look good in tie-dye. After the sermon, I couldn't get out of there fast enough. They were nice people, but they weren't *my* people. I decided that if I couldn't fit in at this rainbow church with my female partner, I was doomed to never belong anywhere.

Then, we walked into a congregational church, and I was prepared to be underwhelmed. Reverend Gary McCann started his sermon by reading scripture, and my eyes were already starting to glaze over. When he finished, he closed his Bible and said, "What does that even mean?" Then he interpreted the verse from two perspectives: Christian and atheist. When he questioned its meaning, he scrambled all my molecules because I had often found myself searching for meaning when forced to memorize Bible verses for tests at school. Rather than blindly following like all the others, Reverend McCann questioned the words in the big book. I later heard this church referred to as a "caring church for thinking people." During that same sermon, he invited us to be critical of scripture, reminding us that much of it was written by man and that Jesus was a critical thinker—as we also should be. Then, he said that atheists and agnostics were welcome. You could almost hear the neurons in my brain firing and rewiring because I had been told unequivocally that nonbelievers bore the devil's clothing. This church had all the species. In the pews sat blacks, whites, browns, gay couples, mixed-race couples, one guy in a tie-dye shirt, and every other representation of the human race you could envision. I had found my tribe.

I believe the universe conspires to unfold in the precise way it is supposed to, and this church was exactly what I needed at this moment in my life. I had been a cop for more than ten years, and without realizing it, I discovered that I had fallen into one of my

calloused moods that a lot of police officers find themselves fend-
ing off. I hadn't realized I was in the middle of this mindset until
one Sunday during a sermon when Reverend McCann talked about
names. It takes a lifetime to grow into the names we're given at
birth. The names we answer to when called on. The names that form
the core of our identity. We are much more than the labels given to
us, he said. Our names set us apart as individuals. As I absorbed his
words, my mind retraced my Norwegian roots, and I had a warm
thought about my own name and how I'd grown into it. I thought
about my quest to trace my maiden name back to my ancestors in
Norway and determine when and why a hyphen was added to Kjen-
dal-Olsen. But deeper into the sermon, it became clear that the
message was more than about surnames. Reverend McCann talked
about the labels we affix to *people* before we even know their names.

Because of the negative mindset I was in, I connected with
Reverend McCann's words from a police perspective. A negative outlook is natural given that we learn early in our careers
that people are capable of heinous acts. This might sound like an
excuse to justify clinging to our callousness, but the psychology
of this outlook is simple. The result of interacting with people
who break the law every day starts to brainwash us into believing that law-abiding citizens are the minority. I got used to being
lied to on the street, so I started to distrust all people. I grew up
fearing the repercussions of lying and violating the Commandments, so when I became a cop, I thought the same God-fearing
moral compass that I had lived in others. It took only weeks to
reprogram my belief that the people I met on the street lived by
the Ten Commandments. I learned quickly that telling a fib was
the least of the transgressions people made. I learned that people

do horrific things to one another and that my wearing a uniform made me an instant enemy.

When Reverend McCann said that we tend to label others without seeing their humanity, I couldn't help but think of all the times I had done that throughout my career. Because we often judge what we don't understand—all people are guilty of this—I struggled to find compassion for those who didn't follow the rules. Again, this played in tune with my upbringing. I believed people were either good or bad, so I had a low tolerance for those who broke the law. I labeled them "criminals" in the same way people paint cops with a broad brush.

Then, I got assigned by my chief to review cases and recommend approval for drug court. Drug court was a referral program, and if someone was found eligible, they would go through a court-supervised rehabilitation program rather than jail. My job was to decide who went where. I had to determine whether the crime committed was driven by drug addiction or they were just criminals who used drugs on top of committing crimes. Even if the criminal offense is the same, there is a difference in what drives the act. Addicts will commit robbery, theft, burglary, etc. in order to get proceeds to feed their addiction. Nonaddicts commit crimes for other reasons that do not include buying drugs. One might assume that as a result of my dad's addiction, I would have had more compassion for those who suffer from a similar affliction, but I didn't. It was the opposite for me—I had little tolerance because I was convinced it was a choice. This conviction made me a terrible person to review these files.

That's how I learned about Scott. He was a twentysomething heroin addict who had a felony record for possession, and he stole from his own family. He stole and sold anything he could get his hands on, so his parents (who allowed him to stay with them after his wife kicked him out) finally decided to press charges. To me, Scott wore the labels *addict* and *felon*, but then I interviewed his family and learned he was more than that. He was a mechanic by trade, but he had lost his job, his wife, and his home to addiction. Before he had become addicted to heroin, he had been a gifted trumpet player. When I interviewed Scott, he could hardly remember just being Scott because all anyone saw was a heroin addict, the track mark scars on his arms a reminder that the past could never be erased completely.

Scott successfully completed drug rehabilitation court, and as of this writing, he's been clean for years. I don't know what it's like to have an addiction that takes over your life and pushes out the good things in it like family and friends and trumpet playing, but hearing his story makes me think twice before putting people in boxes. I spent my adult years being pissed off at my dad for choosing the bottle over his family, yet I remember another side of him that was good. Like my dad, Scott was a good man fighting the demon of addiction. Scott came out on the other side stronger because he owned his story and was provided the chance to tell it. But how often do we assign a label without looking beyond it? All of us are more than our vices and outward appearance, yet those are the badges we wear. Delving into the drug court case files made me realize that people are neither all good nor all bad. It became clear to me that everyone had a story, so I began having conversations with people and asking questions.

In the middle of Reverend McCann's sermon, I realized that the labels pinned on people can lead to horrific acts of violence.

When human beings are labeled and judged because of their appearance, race, culture, or <insert thing here>, it can lead to hatred-fueled attacks. Most of us don't go around physically injuring one another, but we commit emotional "drive-bys" every time we cast judgment on someone or by turning our backs. I subscribe to the notion that when people are labeled, they tend to fulfill that prophecy and align with those labels. Perhaps, if we spent less time affixing labels and more time learning about the people behind the labels, we would begin to see that we are all complex beings, and our thoughts and actions are extensions of our experiences. But most significantly, our struggles are what make us more alike than different. We criticize what we don't understand, and lack of understanding can lead to a belief that the other person is wrong or less than. When you lean into someone else's story, it's difficult to hate. If you want to become more curious about others and don't know where to begin, start by simply asking, "What's your name?"

As I trudged through my career and my personal life, I wasn't always afforded the same benefit. I started to get more comfortable in my skin by being authentically me. I made peace with the fact I wasn't a stereotypical cop and the more content I became with being different, the more uncomfortable it made others. As a new sergeant, I worked for a patrol lieutenant named Mark Hamden, who couldn't have been more different from me. His leadership style, his personality, and his outlook on life starkly contrasted mine. I was conducting roll call with the officers at the beginning of the shift, and the lieutenant was sitting in the back of the room as he did every day. Just as depicted on *Hill Street Blues*, all of the officers assemble in a room, and a sergeant stands at a

podium providing them with information they need before hitting
the street. And yes, the sarge says, "Let's be careful out there" or
something like that famous line as he or she dismisses them. The
lieutenant was a presence in the room both because of his rank
and because he was notorious for his unapproachable demeanor.

After roll call, he summoned me to his office, closed the door,
and told me he didn't like the way I conducted roll call. I must
have had a look of confusion or disbelief because he followed up
with, "I don't like the light atmosphere with the officers. That's
not how a sergeant should act." I found his criticism perplexing.
In my roll call, there was always friendly banter, and I encouraged
participation from the officers instead of just talking at them. But
every good leader must be a good follower, so I nodded my head
in agreement and walked out of his office. From that point on,
I vowed to do better. For the next few weeks, I put on my game
face—the face I usually reserved for the street when things were
serious. I tried to be stern and matter of fact when delivering the
information and giving out assignments. I must have succeeded
because many officers inquired whether something was wrong
with me. They said I wasn't acting like myself. One of the officers
actually asked whether my dog had died.

That's because I *wasn't* being myself. I was being a boss who
was talking *at* people and not *with* them. It wasn't authentic, and
it was no different from the fake street personality I devised as
a patrol officer and the fake domestic spouse I tried to be in my
marriage. It was all too familiar, and I was starting to fall into the
same pattern of losing myself to what someone else expected of
me. When I worked up the nerve, I marched into Lt. Hamden's
office and asked, "When I conduct roll call, am I getting the job

done? Am I sharing information, training, and bulletins? Am I doing the job of a sergeant?"

He paused. "Well, yes."

I responded, "If it's not my performance but my delivery, with all due respect, you cannot create me in your own image."

I held my breath and waited for his response. Silence. As I look back on that moment, I secretly wonder from where that surge of courage came. It was risky (to say the least) to confront a lieutenant like that, and I was certain that I was committing career suicide by confronting him. But since I had his full attention and there was no turning back, I went on to share my philosophy that the more positivity and laughter I could add to our environment, the better our officers would feel. I expounded, "I don't know what kind of day they had before they walked into roll call, and since our moods are manifest in the way we treat the citizens, I'd rather they hit the street feeling happy instead of agitated." Officers are human beings, and when they leave the station feeling heavy with everything they're carrying, all it takes is one bad interaction to ignite a short fuse. I've lost count of how many times I've been called all of the words unfit for print by irate people on the street. While insults are common, they can get under your skin if you aren't careful. Combine that with an already tense or cranky officer, and things could go bad. A minor offense can lead to a major incident when a police officer's actions are out of alignment with the Constitution and basic humanity.

Lt. Hamden didn't respond to my sermon, so I figuratively stepped down from my soapbox, awkwardly thanked him, and walked out. He didn't say a thing. I didn't know how to proceed, so I reverted to what I knew: being me again. He sat in the back of roll call as usual, but he never asked me to change my delivery again.

Years later, I ran into him at a social event after he retired and told him how much I appreciated his allowing me the space to be different despite his not agreeing. He responded simply and true to form: "What you said made sense." And that was it. A heart and mind changed through influence and conviction. That says a lot about him as a person—that he could allow himself to see someone outside his template and accept it.

TEMPLATES ARE MAN-MADE

Throughout my career, I have been underestimated. From the moment I earned my badge, I'd show up on a call and people would say, "You're too little to be a cop" or "Do they let you ride by yourself in a squad car?" As I moved up the ranks, I was often asked, "Do those men follow you?" I have learned to shrug it off or retort with a witty comeback. I never got angry because I tried to respect the templates for which those people saw the world that made them doubt me. It made me try harder to disprove their worldview.

Where do these templates come from? Mine comes from being a child of an alcoholic cop, spending my childhood in a bar, going on to choose a male-dominated profession, and accidently discovering I was gay. Obviously, the lens in which we view the world is formulated by our experiences. Our templates are who we are. Certainly, there are norms of decorum that clearly delineate bad behavior from good, but why do we expect others to conform to the image we've constructed for ourselves rather than allow them to live their own truths? It's a struggle to go against the norm; it's much easier to live in the contrived notion of what others believe a chief, a captain, a CEO, a president, a board member, a wife, or a mother should be. Throughout my entire life, I have been judged for being something or not being something based on someone else's template.

This is a recurring theme in my life. Just this year, I was interviewing for a police chief's job. The interview consisted of a dinner with the eight candidates and the city leadership (human resources and the city managers), four panels with special interest groups, and a final interview with the leadership staff. In the final interview, one of the males on the panel asked me how I handled the media. This is a great question because a police department and the journalists that cover policing need to have mutual respect. In my answer, I explained the relationships I've cultivated with the media and how being transparent with them builds trust. He cut me off in the middle of my answer and said, "That's not what I meant." Perplexed, I waited for him to explain, and he went on to say, "You are a very confident person, and I can see that, but if I were to give you advice, I'd tell you to tone it down." Tone it down. The words punched me in the throat. For some ridiculous reason, I apologized: "Gosh, I'm so sorry if my passion for policing and my ideas come off as too much, but I love this profession, and I get excited about it." I don't know what he said after that, because I checked out. I finished answering the questions, left that interview, and grappled internally. Am I too much? Do I need to tone it down? Then I got pissed. I started thinking about all my male chief colleagues across the nation. I immediately thought of Art Acevedo. He's been the police chief of Austin, Houston, and Miami, and I have been at a dinner party with him and noted how he boisterously entertains and commands a room. I've seen him in front of the microphone with the press where he is yelling and impassioned. And I bet no one has ever told him to "tone it down." The quote from Marianne Williamson flashed into my consciousness: "Your playing small does not serve the world. There is nothing enlightened about shrinking so that other people won't feel insecure around you."

I had no intention of shrinking to fit their template. When I received feedback from the search firm representative, he shared that the city manager said I was "a lot." I knew at that exact moment that I would be pulling out of consideration for the position because I had no intention of toning it down. I knew I wasn't a good fit and decided not to play small. Thanks, Marianne.

Lt. Hamden had a template of what he thought a sergeant should be, and I didn't fit. The guy in the chief's interview thought I was too much. I've never really molded to the norm, but I understand how powerful the judgment can be when we don't act as someone believes we should act.

I refuse to succumb to a contrived template that someone else has formulated. We should be more concerned with results. Are we getting the job done? That should be the litmus test and should matter more than anything else. What's wrong with adding personality in everything we do? What is wrong with being different? If you aren't hurting anyone in the process, break free from the shackles of the social constraints that others have placed on you.

Perception is powerful, but it is not reality. I don't have time to correct all the inaccurate perceptions about me. Over the years, I have had to endure the stereotypes and templates built by others. No, I don't look like a cop. I don't necessarily look how some think a chief should. And I certainly don't have a stoic demeanor until it is required of me in dire situations. I advocate people being exactly who they are in all circumstances. Outside of times that require us to be stoic, we should be exactly who we are. No matter what role in our lives, when it's time to put our game faces on, we always do.

YOU BE YOU

When I was up for the position of commander in my police department, I was competing against ten other lieutenants for the job. I heard rumors that one of my colleagues was opining loudly about how undeserving I was for the position. This wasn't a surprise to me because this guy was a tormentor throughout my entire career. I never worked with him as an officer, but I worked for him when he became a sergeant. Then I worked for him as a lieutenant, and I learned very quickly what an incompetent leader he was. He was known as one of the bad bosses who didn't like being questioned. When he was in charge of the SWAT team, a few officers went to him and respectfully asked for clarification about a decision he had made. He exploded, claiming they had "ambushed" him. I remember thinking how pathetic it was to feel ambushed when your people questioned a decision. He was one of the ones who frequently made it on my who-not-to-emulate list if I ever got into a position of rank.

As my next promotion approached, the saboteurs were in full force, and this lieutenant was among them. He was constructing a plot to get me disciplined over a nonexistent infraction, and my allies in the department informed me of the details. I was exhausted from walking the tightrope with this lieutenant and his regime of evil idiots, so I asked him to meet with me, and he agreed. It was just he and I in a little office, and I pointed out

the obvious: we were not friends. I choose my friends very purposefully, and he wouldn't make the list given that his attributes
conflicted with those I found to be worthy. And I'm certain that I
wouldn't be atop of his list either. I told him what I had heard from
gossip rumblings, and while I was in the middle of talking, I honestly had no idea what I hoped to accomplish in this interaction.
But I kept talking anyway. I told him that I believed he thought
me less worthy of being promoted than he was because of the different trajectories in our careers. He was a gang guy and a SWAT
guy, so his path at the Aurora Police Department was tactical. I
told him that was admirable because I genuinely believe that. But
my path was different in that I was a community policing officer,
a domestic violence detective, and I have taught classes on conflict resolution and leadership. I'm project and people oriented.
I didn't bother going through my resume, but I tried to impress
upon him that his area of expertise did not make him more deserving of this position. Some people (both inside and outside of our
law enforcement) think you can only be a cop if you wear cam-
ouflage and put gun oil in your coffee. Logical people understand
that a vast spectrum of individual skills and specializations cor-
relate to a great organization. I was proud of what I contributed
to our police department, and I knew I was just as worthy as him.
And I let him know.

After I finished my speech, he acknowledged my words and
even conceded that I was accurate in my assessment. I softened
my demeanor because I hadn't expected that he would be so agree-
able, and I thought maybe there was a decent person trapped
inside him after all. We parted ways but not before I wished him
luck and advised him that if he was awarded the commander

position, I would work as hard as I could for him.

There is a danger in minimizing a person because they don't fit your contrived template. His image of me was likely influenced by his template of policing and the data he'd collected about me. Over the years, he and his regime of like-minded men were my tormentors, doing everything they could to write me up or withhold things from me. I wasted energy wondering why they didn't like me until I had the revelation that I didn't like them either. They weren't good leaders, and based on how they treated others, I am not convinced they were good human beings. I became a better leader because they taught me what not to do.

About a week later, my chief called me into his office to announce I had been chosen for the commander position. He pushed his hand toward me, and I don't remember pressing palms because I was in a fog, but I know it happened. I walked out of his office but ran into the women's locker room and hyperventilated in the bathroom stall, trying to wrap my head around being a commander in my police department. My chief rewarded those who didn't fit the "template," and he promoted based on diversity of thought and experience. My chief was a SWAT guy and had more in common with the lieutenant who looked down on me, but the chief saw the value in surrounding himself with people who weren't exactly like him. I see now what a profound gift he gave to me through that lesson, and I will carry it with me always.

My chief understood what so many chiefs before him didn't: it is easy to predict promotions. I worked for five chiefs throughout my career, and four out of five promoted their friends to the commander positions. It was almost comical how obvious it was, yet it was the reality. They promoted those who acted and thought like them. Dee Hock, the founder and former CEO of the Visa credit card association, said, "Never hire or promote in your own image. It is foolish to replicate your strength and idiotic to replicate your weakness." Hock's advice seems logical, yet people continue to bring others along because they mimic their way of thinking. It's natural for us to surround ourselves with people who align with our values and thought processes because it takes less energy to stay within the confines of our own likeness. And it feels good to be validated.

The problem with having no one to question our beliefs or decisions is that it can leave us with the false impression that our way is the right way and that all our decisions are good—heck, even great! We do it every day when it comes to our convictions, believing something so strongly that we expose ourselves only to the people and ideas that support our position, as though that somehow proves we are right.

This lesson applies to the workplace and every place in between. If you have a career, don't assume everyone wants one. If you stay home with your kids, don't judge those who work full time. If you choose not to get married or have kids, that is your prerogative, and you shouldn't have to feel judged or interrogated by those who couldn't imagine an existence without marrying or procreating. Don't walk around applying the templates of your life to someone else's because they simply won't fit. Every person is entitled to determine and recalculate one's journey. If you aren't hurting someone in the process, create your own path with your own tribe and your own vibe.

CHAPTER FIFTEEN

TORMENTORS AND SNIPERS

I have been fortunate to have had many mentors in my life and my career. Mentors become your "theys"—the people who care about you and want to see you succeed. Mentors guide and support you but also tell you the hard truths when you need to hear them. Mentors want to help you improve, not knock you down. Mentors are rare and wonderful, and when I look back, I know the only reason I have achieved what I have is because a small group of people has guided me with a firm but gentle hand. Unfortunately, I've had just as many tormentors. Tormentors are the people who try to thwart your efforts. Sometimes, they are people in your inner circle who simply don't support and encourage your dreams. Other times, they sabotage your efforts. Over the years, I learned that people devote a lot of time and resources to blocking your path when they think of you as a threat.

When I was seventeen, one of my female idols was Kendra. She was two years older than me and an athlete at my high school. When she became a police cadet, I almost fainted because I knew that was going to be my path as well. She had no clue who I was, but I watched her from afar, certain that I would join the police department, and we would become best friends. All of that happened—except the best friend part. She had what could be described as an indifference to me. When I was hired as a cadet, she had already become an officer. On a ride-along with her, she wasn't engaging, and she didn't even try to mentor me, which was my expectation. I felt deflated because she had treated me as invisible. I quickly let go of my dream of palling around like Cagney and Lacey and went on with my life. After the ride-along, I didn't think much of her because our paths didn't cross in the department or in social circles.

I became a sergeant before her, and I had no idea she was not particularly pleased about it. I only found out after someone told me she was using unkind words about me in my absence. Not one to shy away from confrontation, I penned an email to her advising that I heard what she had said about me and asked whether I'd done something to offend her in the last ten years. My theory was that I had, and I figured she might as well tell me so I could apologize. As it turns out, she readily admitted that she resented me for getting promoted to sergeant first and felt she was more deserving because she'd been there longer. She was upset that I had achieved this milestone before she had and offered that she felt I was immature. As I read her response, I remember feeling angry and defensive initially.

Then, a feeling of compassion washed over me because she had focused so much on what she felt my shortcomings were instead of looking inward to her own. Her default was to compete with me, and I was so busy concentrating on my own career that I didn't even notice her. The sad part is that she had no idea how much I admired and looked up to her when I started with the department. It was my first lesson in understanding that not everyone wants the best for you. While I was putting her on a pedestal as a role model, she was busy trying to make sure she didn't share space there. That is when I started putting people in categories of mentors and tormentors, sadly succumbing to the very labels I've grown to despise. In my defense, expounding energy to try and win over my tormentors never seemed to work. From Kendra, I received another lesson in what not to do. When I finally became an officer, I made myself available to the new female cadets who asked to ride with me, and as I moved up in rank, I made it my mission to mentor and support other women. As it turns out, this was still a foreign concept for others, and I would continue to feel the pain and lack of reciprocity throughout my entire career. I can recall so many times as a young officer and a young sergeant when I reached out to other women in rank to get advice and support only to be deflated when they didn't bother to return my call or email. Now that I'm a chief, I understand how busy life and work can get, but *no one* is ever too busy to provide advice or feedback.

After being deflated by Kendra, a heartbreaking pattern began to emerge. I also was enamored of a police officer named Karen, who started her policing career in the early '70s with my dad. I used to see her driving around in her squad car when I was a kid, and I knew I wanted to be just like her. Although my dad was a cop, it meant something to me as a young girl to see a woman in uniform because that is who I wanted to be. After I graduated from the police academy, I reported to the police department to begin the field training program. It consisted of four months of riding with a different field training officer (FTO) each month, so when I saw Karen on my list of FTOs, I was giddy!

I breezed through my first month with my training officer, Kip, and began my second month with Officer Karen. We were assigned to the day shift, and every day around the same time, she drove to her house, which was in her district, and left me in the squad to study my map book or write a report while she enjoyed a coffee break. I didn't think much of it during the first week because I assumed it was part of her training regimen with recruits. Because my first FTO and I prattled about everything, and he invited me to dinner with him and his wife, Karen's formality and all-business attitude were confusing. I started to feel that familiar feeling of disappointment from my female role model. When Karen reviewed my ratings with me at the end of every shift, I received good marks, so I knew her aloofness wasn't because my performance was lacking. For the next three weeks, we repeated the same routine. We answered calls, she left me in the car alone while she took a coffee break—I would have really enjoyed a cup of coffee—and we went home.

We didn't engage in any meaningful conversation, so I was beginning to think it was me. Every morning during roll call, Karen laughed and interacted with the male officers and recruits, but she was cold to me. At the end of our third week of training, I spent my two days off festering, which was an unhealthy mindset for me ahead of the final week of training. After that weekend, when Karen asked me to drive to her house for her routine coffee break, I lost my shit. Parked in front of her house, I ranted about how well I was doing in the program, but it was obvious she didn't like me; that I was sick of sitting in the car alone and couldn't understand why she wouldn't speak to me; and how I wanted coffee, too! What the hell? She got out of the car without saying anything, quickly returned with a thermos, and told me to drive. I knew I had blown it. I had just screamed at an FTO, and she was clearly going to flunk me out of the program—I was sure we were going back to the department to meet with the sergeant. Instead, she asked me to pull over. I pulled into a park entrance with a view of the river, and I turned the car off and faced forward. She pulled out a cup, poured coffee in it from the thermos, and handed it to me. I looked at her, and she poured herself a cup. "I want to tell you a story," she said.

The French vanilla coffee was strong and hot, and I was so glad to have it that I cupped it with both hands and sipped while she talked. She said she started policing in the early '70s, and when she went to the academy, none of the male recruits spoke to her. She ate alone at the long cafeteria table and endured silence during the entire time she spent there. She came back and was met with the same resistance from the officers at the police department. Her voice cracked when she told me how she would find sanitary napkins in her mailbox and stuck to her squad car as a twisted way to send the message that she was unwanted. She told me that officers wouldn't back her up on calls. She spent years with her head down just trying to do her job while never feeling as though she belonged or was accepted. So, when I walked in as a seventeen-year-old cadet, she noted that I was immediately accepted, and she said that bothered her. And now that I was a twenty-one-year-old recruit sitting in her car, she acknowledged that she felt resentment toward me for "having it so easy."

I never felt unwelcome or unwanted when I walked into the police department. I was confident, excited, and engaged with all the officers because I asked questions, and now looking back, I realize I had probably been annoying. But she was right. They accepted me, and as the only woman in my group of six cadets, I never once felt that I didn't belong. I sat there soaking in all her words in silence. I tried to imagine how it must have felt to be the first woman in the department. Not only did she have to endure being in the out-group; she had to absorb hatred and hostility from her fellow officers.

I remember a long silence in the car with Karen as I tried to formulate words from all the thoughts I was having. I finally spoke, and the first thing I said was, "I wish you could see you the way I see you." I went on to tell her how excited I used to get as a little girl seeing her driving around the west side of Aurora. Then I told her that the reason I and other women had been accepted into the culture of the police department was because of her. Before we showed up, there wasn't a welcome mat for us. In fact, there was no path at all, and the first women in policing were the ones who hacked and clawed their way through to forge a path for the rest of us. I told her that her tenacity and resilience were the reasons the rest of us could walk into the profession at all.

At that moment, I understood the power of "firsts." The majority of Karen's career was met with hardship and sabotage, yet she didn't quit. She pressed on and developed a bulletproof resilience that was evident when I looked at her. After that moment, I think she gained a new perspective as well. Instead of resenting the fact that women coming into the profession were accepted, she needed to own her role in that progress. After that moment, she didn't leave me in the squad anymore. She invited me in, and I spent those coffee breaks during our last week together with her and her husband, talking and laughing as she taught me how to be a police officer. Karen went on to become the first female sergeant in the history of our police department. The day she was promoted, and I saw her in her crisp white shirt with her brand-new chevrons, I cried. She had done something monumental by crashing through what we call the "brass ceiling" in policing. I was over the moon.

She died a short time later after being diagnosed with breast cancer. I wish Karen was still here because if she was, I would remind her every day of her courage and her legacy. Not only did I become a police officer because I saw her doing it, but I knew I could move up in my organization because she did. I secretly hoped Karen was looking down when I was being sworn in as chief because I credit my success to her will never to give up.

Without even realizing it, Sgt. Karen was my role model. She was living her life as a cop in the '70s with no idea that a little girl was watching and wishing to be like her. I think of that often when other women reach out to me and tell me they want to be police officers or when women from other agencies reach out to meet for advice on navigating promotions in their agencies.

LESSONS FROM FAILING

When I put in for the position of superintendent of the Chicago Police Department at the end of 2019, I got a harsh reminder yet again that life is filled with tormentors. The Chicago Police Board president called to inform me, along with the other finalists, that I was in the running for the job. As a result, the finalists' names went public, and a firm began a comprehensive background check on me. I would expect nothing less, and as a cop for nearly twenty-seven years, I was confident nothing in my background would be an impediment—that is, until I was sitting in my interview with Chicago mayor Lori Lightfoot. As she thumbed through a big file, she asked me to tell her about a conference I attended in 2011 or 2012. She said it was in Texas, and someone reported that I was at a bar dancing "provocatively" with a man. As I sat there in my starched power suit, I almost burst out laughing as I tried to recall the time. "Yes," I said. I did recall that conference. I had been a board member of the National Association of Women Law Enforcement Executives (NAWLEE), and after our business meeting, we went to a bar to socialize. I had a few "margs," and I was dancing, as were a lot of conference attendees. I told the mayor that I was most likely guilty of terrible dancing, but I didn't recall the provocative moves that were reported. It seemed to me that this question was one my male competition would never have been asked, even if they had been pole-dancing at a conference.

As I was driving home from that interview, the magnitude of the act of sabotage hit me. It was circa 2020, yet fellow tribe members from a *women's* law enforcement organization came forward to report this deplorable behavior from nine years earlier! I tried to think of a time when I would go out of my way to thwart another person for something so petty. After the process was over, I discovered that one of the people who reported my alleged dirty dancing was a retired female officer from the LAPD. She had been one of the "firsts" in Los Angeles to achieve rank, yet she went out of her way to sabotage my advancement. The irony of having a fellow woman from NAWLEE attempt to block my path was both humorous and pathetic to me, but I wasn't surprised by it at all. It reinforced for me that tormentors are alive and well, and in my quiet moments, I am grateful that I am not wired to harm others. If I saw a woman doing something that I thought would be harmful to herself or her career, I would offer her gentle redirection, and I would help to straighten her crown. Mayor Lightfoot ultimately chose David Brown for the superintendent's position, but I'm pretty sure it wasn't because of my sexy dancing.

A year later, I was called upon to apply for another chief's position in the city of Nashville. My maternal grandmother was born there, so I felt some roots. It is a bustling city with lots of personality, and I was a big country music fan growing up, so it checked the box for the location. From a police perspective, I knew there were a lot of challenges in the city and within the police department, so the thought of rolling up my sleeves there made me excited. Keep in mind, being invited to apply is simply that—an invitation. Firms who conduct chief searches have a pretty good sense of the talent in the profession, but ultimately, the decision resides with the mayor or city manager. Just as I had for Chicago, I first consulted Aurora mayor Richard Irvin. For the opportunity in Chicago, he was the one who had told me I'd be crazy not to go for it. He provided the same support for Nashville. Richard told me he didn't want me to go but understood my wanting to spread my wings. I will never forget his leadership and friendship during that time in my life. Despite his blessing, I felt apprehensive because my officers and citizens were very supportive of Chicago but might not have supported my applying for a job out of state. Some of my male mentors pointed out to me that while my default was to worry about my city and my people, I needed to be unapologetic about wanting to challenge myself in a major city. The loyalty I have to my Aurora tribe is indescribable, but I have no reason to feel guilty after dedicating nearly thirty years to my police department and my hometown.

What was the worst thing that could happen if I went for it? For me, it had nothing to do with not getting the job. The worst case would be not getting the job and having people believe I had turned my back on my department. I decided that I would be willing to accept a failure and ultimately the backlash because I knew that most reasonable people understood my ambition and desire for a new landscape. So I applied. The more I became immersed in researching Nashville, the more I wanted that job. The city had the kinds of problems I wanted to solve: crime and culture. I was chomping at the bit to get in there and unleash the talent and skill of the cops who were passionate about progress. The Nashville mayor ultimately opted for the only internal candidate who had applied. Before I had a chance to process the rejection, the local paper's headline read, "Aurora's Top Cop Not Chosen for Nashville Police Chief Position."

In both of those jobs, I felt as though I failed publicly. I made the mistake of reading comments on social media, where the tormentors and haters did not disappoint. They cowardly hid behind their computer screens and clicked away like keyboard warriors. And for a moment, it got to me because just as I feared, I was accused of not being loyal to Aurora. Then, I realized those people posting didn't even know me, so I reminded myself of my "theys" once again. I pictured the haters sitting behind their computers doing nothing meaningful themselves, and I started laughing at how insignificant they were. I also realized that I was better for having gone through those rigorous processes because I learned so much, and I'm damn proud to have made it as a finalist in two major city police departments. In my estimation, I'm the winner at losing.

DON'T YOU SAY NEVER TO ME

I have never competed against anyone in my life. This sounds like an odd declaration given the illustrations of sabotage I've offered and the jobs I've not been awarded. It's true that there are invariably fewer and fewer positions the higher you move up in an organization. Yet I have never looked over at the people next to me and compared myself to them. As a woman in a male-dominated field, it was useless to waste my time trying to go toe to toe with the men around me. That doesn't mean they were faster or stronger; it just feels like comparing apples to coconuts. It doesn't work.

That's the advantage of being different: you just get used to the idea of it, and pretty soon, you stop looking for similarities in others and try to get better at what you do. Unfortunately, others don't necessarily hold the same philosophy. One of the hardest lessons I've ever had to learn is that people relentlessly and ruthlessly attempt to chop you off at the knees for them to get ahead. It is admittedly more difficult to have women tormentors because there are so few of us in law enforcement that you'd think we might stick together. As the stories in this chapter have illustrated, sticking together is sadly not the norm. But to keep things in proper balance, I've had no shortage of male tormentors.

It's not as important to give the details of the events as it is to delve into the lessons learned about competition. On one hand, the messages we hear are very clear. Crush your competition. Win at all costs. In the book *The 48 Laws of Power*, Robert Greene uses anecdotes from history to outline the ways to become powerful, and in most of the examples, the lesson is to play dirty and manipulate others to get what you want. This book was suggested to me after one of my tormentors continued to quash my efforts. After I read it, I was acutely aware of the handbook for destruction. Even though I refused to play, it was interesting to learn the rules of the game.

I'm embarrassed to admit that I've been naive to the notion of sabotage. I'm sure it's because I don't view everyone as a threat, but I have now learned that everyone is your friend until you find yourself in competition with them—or they with you. For the first fifteen years of my career, I got along with nearly everyone. While I learned from the great bosses and emulated them after I became a sergeant, I studied the bad bosses and vowed never to be like them. My mantra was to be the kind of sergeant I would want to have. That's it. It wasn't about becoming a carbon copy of someone else. Rather, it was about absorbing the qualities I admired into who I already was.

I was five years into being a sergeant and looking ahead to taking the lieutenant's test. I was getting great performance reviews, and I believed I had a chance at becoming the first female in the history of my department to achieve the rank of lieutenant. My tormenter sat two levels up and had his eye on the pawns—the only way to keep me from gaining a higher position on the board was obviously to block my move. He called me into his office, telling me that he had just finished reading the annual evaluations I'd written on each officer in my squad and felt my narratives were too "cheerleady." I was confused as I had provided feedback to my officers by giving them positive reinforcement in what they had done well, as well as areas upon which they needed to improve. I told the commander that I wanted to acknowledge my officers' strengths rather than concentrate solely on their weaknesses. He said he thought that I was "soft," so I pushed back. There was nothing soft about building people up rather than knocking them down, I said. I could see my explanation infuriated him. "You will never become a lieutenant in this police department if I can help it," he blurted out.

I was stunned. This was my commanding officer with all the power telling me I would never get promoted, so I felt as though I had been punched in the throat. I remember feeling the sting of tears beginning to form, but I would not allow him the satisfaction of seeing me upset. I walked out of his office and went to my car to cry tears of anger, frustration, and hatred toward him. I started believing his words and wondering if he was right—maybe I wasn't cut out to be a lieutenant. Then I got pissed again, and something in me snapped. I knew I didn't respect him as a person or a leader, so I questioned why I allowed him to get inside my head for that short time. My entire attitude shifted, and I channeled my inner Ruth, a character from Fannie Flagg's book *Fried Green Tomatoes at the Whistle Stop Cafe* when she looked at Idgie and said, "Don't you ever say never to me."

Ignoring my commander's ridicule, I started reading all the books assigned in preparation for the lieutenant's promotional exam. Whenever I got tired of reading, his face would flash in my head, and I pressed on. I finished the books, and I read them again.

Then I dictated them on a recorder and played the tape back when I drove or worked out. I learned the material inside and out, and when I finished taking the test, I was confident that I did well in the entire process. I scored number one on that lieutenant's list and became the first female in the history of my police department to reach that rank. *Don't you ever say never to me.* When you learn to use criticism as fuel, you will never run out of energy.

I went on to become a commander and moved into the office next to my tormentor, which gave me great satisfaction. Nearly six years later, four people from my agency applied for the chief's job when the position opened. That same commander who told me I'd never become a lieutenant was one of them. He told me he didn't really want the position, but he was going to put in for it. Instead of saying he was going all in and wanted the job, he downplayed it, so if he didn't get it, he could ultimately fall back on not wanting it in the first place. His was a common refrain for promotions or positions: "I didn't really study" or "I didn't want the job, so I didn't try." I've never understood why people just don't call it what it is: a failure! Own it. Say you wanted and you tried to get it, but you fell short. There is nothing wrong with that! We all have tried and failed—it's what connects us as humans.

Despite his declaration, I knew he wanted that position badly. He needed that position because it was his only shot. He never went back to school to get more education. He didn't do anything to prepare, so if he didn't get the job, there were no other options for him but to remain as commander. That probably would have been acceptable to him if it wasn't me who got the job. I, on the other hand, wanted the job and made no secret about it. I told everyone I was putting in for it and was excited about it.

I even walked into the office of Lieutenant Keefe Jackson to tell him I thought he would make a great chief and should apply for the position. I respected him immensely and knew he would be an amazing chief. He politely declined because I was putting in for it, but I know he would have made an even better chief than I. When I became chief, I made him my deputy chief because he has always made me better.

The difference between me and my tormentor was that I wanted what was best for the police department, even if that meant it wasn't me. Over the years, I'd grown tired of watching egocentric leaders make decisions based on their own self-interest rather than for the organization. From all the data I'd collected over the years, I figured that giving power away and lifting others would change our culture for the better. He, on the other hand, wanted what was best for him and his cronies. I deduced this based on watching his actions, as he used his power to promote his friends and family. Every decision he made was to elevate his like-minded regime and keep others down, leading with fear and punishment, and he did not want me as the top cop because he knew I would be his unraveling. The position wasn't something I wanted so badly that I would knock others off the chessboard to get it, but he would. I know that desperate people do desperate things, but I was not prepared for the depths to which he would go to get what he wanted. I would find out later that he convinced other people to apply for the chief's job to knock me off the board. Backdoor promises were made, and their only mission was for anyone but me to get the job. I was too busy not playing the game to know that I was the object of the game, so honestly, that suited me better.

I knew I was going to be okay if I didn't get the job. I already had a plan B devised. Sitting my family down, I asked them whether they would be willing to leave the state because there were some extremely enticing positions open for chief, and several agencies had already asked me to apply. Failing to get the chief's job in my own department would be disappointing, but my resume of experience would afford me other options. With my family squarely on board, I accepted the outcome, whatever it might be.

I still haven't figured out why they invested so much energy into hating me, but I genuinely don't give a damn. Over time, I have come to enjoy tormentors because they energize me. My tormentors remind me that I compete with only one person in my life: myself. Once I committed to constant self-improvement, a weird and wonderful thing happened. I never missed an opportunity to go to another training class, further my education, or better myself. Pretty soon, my resume was bigger than everyone else's—which positioned me to become the first female lieutenant, commander, and finally, chief in my organization—and all I did was stop looking at what everyone else was doing and concentrate on me. When you do that, all those people who haven't worked as hard as you are in the rearview mirror. And if the people you pass along the way tattle on you for dancing sexy after a few margaritas, own that moment and smile because it was probably worth it.

There is a peace that comes over me when I think of my life and career and how I can confidently say that I never pushed anyone off a pedestal or stepped on anyone to elevate myself. When I think of my tormentors, I take solace in the understanding that something is lacking in them to devote time and energy to thwart my progress. I feel satisfaction in living well and recognizing that it takes far more energy to conspire to knock people down than to offer them a hand and help them up.

Fortunately, both male and female mentors have manifested in my life to help guide me on my path to alert me to the tormentors and snipers. I've been on the receiving end of kindness shown by other females in our profession. At a California chief's conference where I was speaking, Sylvia Moir (chief of El Cerrito, California, at the time) introduced me to a movement called "save a seat for a sister." The concept is simple. When you are attending a conference or a meeting, put your bag down on the seat next to you to save a seat for another female that might walk into the room. When they do, wave them down and tell them you've saved them a seat. It doesn't matter if you've never met them before, you welcome them to your space. We women are so few in numbers, so it is our responsibility to make one another feel welcome. A year or so later, I walked into a meeting at the International Association of Chiefs of Police, and fellow board member Chief Cynthia Renaud waved me over to show me the seat she'd saved for me. I was a new board member, and I cannot begin to explain how much that gesture meant to me. Chief Carmen Best and I recently spoke at NYPD on a panel, and afterward, she pulled me aside and told me my face looked snarly while I was on stage. I have a habit of chewing the inside of my cheek when I'm thinking, and it translates to my looking angry. Every time I start to revert to that bad habit, I think of Carmen caring enough to point it out. When I think of the female saboteurs I've endured, my faith in womanhood is restored because of women leaders like these.

Mentors lift you up, and they care enough about you to help straighten your crown. Remember that you will have both mentors and tormentors, but don't waste your time trying to win over the haters. Focus only on competing with yourself. And most importantly, choose to be the person who helps others straighten their crown rather than the one who tries to knock it off.

CHAPTER SIXTEEN

THE POWER OF SYMBOLS

A career in law enforcement is made up of individual and personal challenges and triumphs. Like any profession, development throughout our careers is a culmination of internal and external factors that play a role. As you have heard, the personal challenges I've endured in the evolution of leadership have been internal. When I became the chief, I discovered that the challenges of running an organization were not only with my personnel, but also the external stakeholders. For most of my career, I enjoyed and reveled in the support from members of the community. Don't get me wrong, I have absorbed anger from crime victims and residents who have been upset with an officer's conduct, but those incidents have been surmountable, and they didn't amount to an overall feeling that the public was against us. It wasn't until George Floyd was murdered that I experienced the visceral disdain for police.

Whoever coined the phrase "Defund the Police" is a genius. When I saw protestors picketing in my city with that motto, I remember feeling defensive because I thought it meant to get rid of cops. I smugly recall thinking, "Good luck with that" because the consequences of a lawless society would be devastating. Societal norms of morality and decorum are unwritten, but policy and legislation succeed in keeping order and protecting people from harm. It's illegal to kill someone if you are mad at them. That's a good rule. When rules and laws are applied equitably, they succeed in keeping people safe. Speed limits, for example, were put in place because people were driving too fast and dying from car accidents. Applying a speed limit reduces fatal accidents. In that same category, since the mandatory seat belt law was instituted, fifteen thousand lives are saved per year. Police officers are charged with enforcing these laws to keep people safe. We also turn to police when we are a victim of a crime because we believe that the law enforcement arm of the criminal justice system will assist us if we've been robbed, beaten, or violated in some way. We trust the process because the alternative is vigilante justice. It's dangerous to take matters into our own hands, and this is illustrated in gang wars, where revenge through retaliation is the norm. Taking away police will result in lawlessness, and that places a community in harm. After I learned that defunding the police actually meant taking financial resources away from police departments and using it instead to fund social workers and other programs, I found it ironic because cops have been asking for this for years. Social ailments like homelessness, mental health issues, substance abuse, truancy, and domestic issues (to name a few) have become the responsibility of law enforcement. If funding other agencies allows experts in those fields to respond and provide resources to solve the root problem, you'll see us protesting with you to defund the police! But don't actually take money away from the police. Ninety percent of my budget in my police department went to personnel, so defunding a police organization won't result in the desired outcome. Leave enforcing the law to cops, and let everyone else handle the other stuff.

I didn't know what ACAB meant until I started seeing hashtags with the acronym after the George Floyd incident. All Cops Are Bastards. I know it's not meant to be funny, but I admit that it makes me laugh. I feel like people can do better when coming up with an insult to the police profession. I am more impressed with "pig" as a derogatory and inflammatory name for police. At least it's accompanied by bacon jokes (which never get old).

When I conducted my research, I learned that ACAB has been around for a long time. Its history can be traced to the first part of the twentieth century when "All Coppers Are Bastards" was abbreviated in the 1940s by workers on strike. I'm not sure why striking unions had a beef with cops, but that appears to be the origin. It resurfaced later in the 1970s by a group of hoodlums who were sick of getting pushed around by cops. That's fair. ACAB began to surface in punk music lyrics, where it took hold and became a battle cry for anarchists and antiestablishment movements. And now it's at peak popularity with the emergence of the anti–police brutality and "resist" movement. Most of the cops I know are against police brutality, so suffice it to say, not all cops are bastards if that's the meaning on which society has settled. But knock yourself out if ACAB is the tattoo you choose to adorn your body with.

Anti-police movements have been around for longer than I have, so I don't take much of it personally. Gallup polls show elected officials and lawyers lower than law enforcement when it comes to confidence, but I've never seen an organized protest against lawyers (I could be wrong about this). Demonstrations and protests against the police and lawmakers are organized efforts to effect change. Let me back up; people protest and demonstrate in favor of or against many topics. We have an abortion clinic in my city, so I have a lot of experience in navigating the emotions surrounding a topic about which someone feels a great deal of passion. I met with the pro-life team of organizers every few months to make sure they were afforded their right to protest. A police officer in uniform is the epitome of neutrality, and it is our job to ensure that people on both sides of the issue are protected. There are many pro-choice police officers who were dedicated to protecting the pro-lifers. And vice versa. I don't care if the protestors are holding ACAB signs; it is the police officer's job to keep them safe. And let me say loudly for the people in the back that there is no excuse for an officer to use any force (less lethal or otherwise) on those peacefully exercising their right to free speech. I have seen videos of cops pepper spraying peaceful protestors, and it is an abhorrent abuse of power. But the moment a bottle or a brick is thrown at the police or the opposing group, a crime has been committed, and it's time to identify and arrest the aggressor. A lone agitator is easy to home in on and swiftly arrest or remove from the crowd. But the problem is that others begin to engage in violence, and when the cops react with a less lethal option, it agitates the crowd, and more violence ensues. But no one should stand by and allow officers to take bricks in the head or bottles of urine thrown at them without a response.

The night of the riots in my city, nearly 250 of our officers responded. My department only had fifty sets of riot gear to protect themselves. I'm no mathmagician, but that doesn't add up to protecting our officers. The demonstrators marched peacefully into our downtown, and the crowd evolved into bad actors who began looting our businesses and setting fire to our squad cars. They broke windows and attempted to steal an ATM machine. They pried up bricks from our city sidewalks and hurled them at our officers. Watching the video of this makes you shudder. We responded in defense by using pepper balls to keep the violent mob at bay, and I won't back down from that decision. Departments all over the nation who incurred unrest experienced the media only rolling footage of officers defending themselves, which made it seem as though the cops were the aggressors. When my department viewed footage in its entirety, we observed the "peaceful" protestors changing into different clothing and retrieving weapons. The same occurred in Chicago, and CPD had the good sense to set up cameras before the protests, where it was unequivocally clear that the protestors provoked the violence. So many of the media outlets choose the footage that puts officers in an unfavorable light despite their being forced to defend and react. Once again, I denounce any officer who uses force that is unnecessary, and good departments have trained and prepared officers on how to handle protests. I don't know any officer in my department who has ever had an issue with protecting peaceful demonstrators. What we do take issue with are people who convert their passion into violence and destruction of property. I don't know how smashing glass windows to gain entry into a business and stealing everything inside helps your movement—whatever that movement may be.

These movements to abolish, defund, and decry the entire police profession are taking a toll on the officers. Forget the bad apples like Derek Chauvin and those like him. I'm talking about the juicy, ripe apples that make up the majority of law enforcement. We need not look far to see the consequences when police officers stand down. Mayhem ensues, and angry mobs destroy property and harm others.

BLACK LIVES MATTER

The Black Lives Matter (BLM) movement was born in 2013 by three female black organizers—Alicia Garza, Patrisse Cullors, and Opal Tometi. The women launched a social justice campaign using the social media hashtag, #BlackLivesMatter, after the acquittal of George Zimmerman in the shooting death of Trayvon Martin back in 2012. The movement grew nationally in 2014 after the deaths of Michael Brown in Missouri and Eric Garner in New York. Since then it has established itself as a worldwide movement, particularly after the death of George Floyd. Most recently, #BlackLivesMatter has spearheaded demonstrations worldwide protesting police brutality and systematic racism that overwhelmingly affects the Black community.

The controversy about BLM stems from what you believe their mission to be. If you associate #BlackLivesMatter as a terrorist organization, you're likely to see this group as a threat. If you see them as a group of impassioned individuals whose mission is to shine the light on police brutality and denounce white supremacy, your paradigm is different. The lines blurred because we saw people with #BlackLivesMatter insignia setting fire to our cities and looting businesses. As a result, people associated the group with violence. I've heard people argue that the movement has done more harm than good because of the left-wing outlets defending and even justifying rioting and looting. The right-wing outlets are quick to assign them the label of agitators. Martin Luther King Jr. was a proponent of nonviolence, yet people saw him as an agitator. This is not different from how people see the Black Lives Matter movement present day.

After days of rioting, I recall hearing the pro-BLM movement justifying looting as a form of reparations for oppression. Nothing in that argument is logical to me. Change happens when people rise together and make noise so loud that they cannot be ignored. I believe in that, so if you wear your BLM swag and you fight peacefully for equity and social justice, you are liberators who are moving in the right direction toward inclusion.

THIN BLUE LINE

In response to "Black Lives Matter," the phrases "All Lives Matter" and "Blue Lives Matter" became a retort. I remember thinking how stupid that was. No one was saying that black lives (or any other lives) were more important. It is not a competition on whose life has more value, and people really seemed to be missing the point. Of course police officers' lives matter. No one ever said they didn't. As a cop, I have never felt that my life was devalued. Naturally, some criminals don't value our lives, and line-of-duty deaths are evidence of this. But the profession is largely supported, and polls showing police satisfaction throughout the years speak to this.

The "thin blue line" dates back to the British infantry regiment in the 1850s called "The Thin Red Line." It was commandeered by police in the 1950s, who began using it to refer to police officers because of their blue uniforms. The evolution of the blue line became a symbol to law enforcement and within the profession; it is often used to adorn and pay homage to those who have died in the line of duty. The thin blue line in a positive light evokes pride in the profession and denotes the blue line of officers who protect our communities. I have lost count of the number of T-shirts I own with the thin blue line symbol, and I wear them proudly because I believe it stands for service, justice, and fundamental fairness.

Somewhere along the way, the thin blue line morphed into signifying an unwritten code of silence used to cover up police misconduct. White supremacy flags have been seen flying next to thin blue line flags, thereby (rightfully) questioning its meaning. Then we saw these same flags being carried by those who stormed the Capitol on January 6. I was furious to see the flag to which I associate service and selflessness being flown while people tried to overthrow the government and our democracy. I recall hearing police officers justifying the sightings of the thin blue line flags at the Capitol insurrection. They didn't associate the flag with violence and doubled down on the thin blue line as what separates the good guys from the bad guys. Nothing in that argument is logical to me. If you wear your thin blue line swag as a noble member or supporter of the law enforcement profession and you fight peacefully and equitably for justice, you are liberators who are moving in the right direction toward inclusion.

If you were paying attention, you have noted that the paragraphs written about BLM and the thin blue line read similarly.

If you think the BLM movement denotes domestic terrorism but think it's okay to storm the Capitol with a thin blue line flag and defy democracy, you are misguided. Those who believe the thin blue line stands for white supremacy but think it's okay to wear a BLM shirt and break windows and set things on fire, you are also misguided.

Symbols are powerful, and history has taught us that they can denote a cause for good or evil. Some people hijack these symbols and use them in defiance of the original intent. When this happens, harm is done to the purity and goodness of what people look to for inspiration and alignment to their passion and mission.

MELONS AND THE SUN

When I was a child, my dad told me that people who are a different color from me were that way because of where they lived in relation to the sun and because of "melons." He said something about the equator and how it determined the pigmentation of a person's skin. He watched a lot of Carl Sagan, and what he had told me sounded a lot like science, so I believed him. I know now that he was saying "melanin," not melons, when he was explaining to me the reasons for our skin color, but I was six, so I get a pass for screwing it up. I didn't understand it at the moment, but I know now what a gift my father gave to me. He was telling me, in essence, that we are all the same on the inside, and our skin tones were relative to our ancestors and their proximity to the equator. He said to me, "When you slice us all open, we are exactly the same." It was a morbid image, but I totally got it.

What might seem like an insignificant lesson for a child may very well have been the most important one he ever gave to me. I grew up looking at people with different skin colors as just that—people with different skin colors. What sounds like an oversimplification is exactly what it should be. He pointed out the differences in our skin but never attached an addendum about one color being superior to another. It was simply different by way of the levels of melon.

When I reflect on this, I understand the "critical race theory" and the notion that race is a social construct. Sometimes I wonder if I'm allowed to feel this passionate despite never having experienced racism personally. I worry that people of color might dismiss me as "not getting it" because I've not felt the pain personally. I've experienced truckloads of sexism, but I know it's not the same. Even so, I feel a genuine visceral reaction at the absurdity of racial disparity. At the risk of revealing what I believe is my own intellectual elitism, I don't understand how people are so ignorant to believe that whites are superior to anyone. Sometimes I wonder if that's half of my problem. Because I can't comprehend it, I don't see the world that way and perhaps I naively assume that others don't either. I have tried to understand prejudice and where it comes from, and I guess it's no different than how I was raised. If my dad taught me that people with different skin color are no different than the vast examples of nature around us, other people's dads probably told them that black and brown people are bad, and just like I believed my dad, they believed theirs. And they grew up to become politicians, lawmakers, doctors, cops, and teachers and so on, and they make policy and business decisions central to their belief that people of color are less than.

The lessons we learn at home are foundational, but they aren't the only institutions and collectives that impact our ideology.

Friends, teachers, and the educational curriculum all shape the way we see the world. We can point to our children's books to validate that black history has been manipulated to offer a sanitized version of what really happened. Our children learn about icons like Rosa Parks and Martin Luther King Jr., but they aren't taught that Black Americans have been fighting for equality for hundreds of years.

I recognize that I've once again oversimplified something very complex, but it helps me understand "systemic racism" through the revelation that racist humans build racist institutions that cultivate racist systems and processes. If you are white, the racist systems and policies exist behind the scenes, so we become oblivious to them. But to those who are not white, racist policies, laws, and institutions are minefields that must be negotiated daily. I wish I could alter the belief system of people who think they are superior by simply explaining the science of the equator and "melons." It's physiology. It's not that hard. And yet it is what divides us because some people truly believe that white people are superior. That mindset, aligned with power of position and institutions, has caused so much harm. And in all my righteous indignation, I am reminded that I am a part of the criminal justice system that historically put more people of color in prison and for longer than white people. I'm part of the problem, and I've gone along this entire time reminding people that you go to jail if you break the law. I never stopped to ponder the disparity of a white kid breaking the law and his sentence versus the black kid.

Where do we go from here as a society and in our respective institutions? In policing, we can start by ensuring that we recruit and hire people who don't exhibit those biases. Sounds easy enough, right? Hire good people. As much effort as we put into background checks, there will inevitably be a few assholes that slip through the cracks. But for the most part, the digital age leaves a person's fingerprint on the world, and we can usually gather data that reveals a person's true self. Once we hire people, we can teach, train, educate, and ultimately alter behavior if we can interrupt the thought pattern of bias, so we recognize what lives within us. Those in leadership positions can set policy that prohibits taking actions based on skin color, gender, orientation, or group affiliation. But let's be honest, those policies are already in place, and I know that there are still bad cops using their position irresponsibly, so we have to create a culture where it's not accepted. I know that that no one in their right mind would exhibit bigoted language or action around me because I wouldn't tolerate it. The people that I choose to spend my time with wouldn't either. So when we (those of us opposed to racial bias) become the majority, the few who are left behind won't have anywhere to practice their behavior. Soon their power will diminish, and we will push them out, and they won't be able to harm anyone else. The powerless will be empowered. We do this by hiring more black cops and more female cops to reflect the demographics of our cities. If the good white cops (currently the majority) decide to speak out against racism and call out actions and behavior of their bigoted brethren, only then will we begin to see a shift in culture.

Speaking out when someone says something disparaging in your presence makes a giant impact. Checking your own thoughts and biases and questioning the crap someone taught you when you were impressionable is a start. Departments who commit to training and talking openly about race and power are the ones who will begin to permeate the culture. Dissecting police use-of-force incidents and asking if a bias might have played a part is a start. Given the amount of power police officers possess, law enforcement should be open to exploring every possibility. If biases do exist, we can identify the behaviors that need to change, as well as the thinking and believing that lead to the behavior.

Black lives do matter. And until every single person can understand that this movement was born because throughout history, black lives didn't matter, we cannot move forward.

CHAPTER SEVENTEEN

LEADERSHIP IS ABOUT DISAPPOINTING PEOPLE

I went to Harvard. That statement is true(ish) because I was fortunate enough to spend three weeks attending the Harvard Kennedy School of Government "Executives in State and Local Government" program. But I still love saying I went to Harvard and pausing before I say, "For three weeks." It was the most academic of the training I've ever attended, and I left there with my mind blown beyond its original dimensions.

The reason it was so good was that the instructors didn't allow you to give a canned answer and then move onto the next person. And, unlike most classrooms, they didn't wait for you to raise your hand. The notion that you could be called upon at any moment to offer your opinion about a discussion or an assigned reading meant that we were all at the ready.

One instructor in particular was terrifying. Marty Linsky would stand in front of the large audience and toss out a cerebral question, and when he scanned the room, I found he normally chose the person to call upon who was attempting to avoid eye contact. I was never that person because I always have something to say, and I'm not usually afraid to say it. But this was different. After someone made a comment, Professor Linsky would gaze at you and press harder. "Why did you answer the question in that way?" Or "What did you mean by that?" Or perhaps, "Why have you come to that conclusion?"

I'm usually good for about one answer that makes me appear of average intelligence, but the more he dug deeper, the more my classmates and I struggled to answer the question. We would often become flustered, but he remained relentless in his pursuit of the "why." At that moment, I wanted to punch him in the throat, but now that I am able to see clearly, he was doing what so many people fail to do: dig deeper for meaning.

I can regurgitate talking points that I've heard from a news correspondent or from a colleague and even feel strongly in alignment with those opinions. But when you start asking seemingly simple follow-up questions, most people can't go beyond their canned answers. It forces you to dig deeper, and when you've hit the bottom, most people find that they know very little about a particular topic.

Marty changed me. He made me do research to support my position, and my greatest motivation was not to look foolish in class. Fortunately, that lesson has transcended the classroom, and

I have learned to carefully construct my position based on facts. I have also learned to challenge my own position. That's my biggest takeaway. When he forced us to peel away the layers after parroting an answer, it actually caused some of us to change the way we looked at something on which we once felt immovable.

But the day Marty literally blew my mind was when he spanned his gaze at all of us and he uttered these words: "Leadership is about disappointing people at the rate they can absorb."

What the hell does that mean? He saw the confusion on everyone's face, and he repeated the same phrase as though the repetition would be cause for enlightenment.

"Leadership is about disappointing people at the rate they can absorb."

Nope. Still nothing, Marty. Leadership is inspiring people to align with a vision. It's about taking people where they need to go but otherwise wouldn't. It's about setting clear goals for your people and getting work done through others. Great leaders do the opposite of disappointing people. Dammit Marty Linsky, you have lost your mind.

I went to Harvard in 2011, and on February 1, 2017, I was sitting at my desk reflecting upon several decisions that I'd made during my one year as the chief of police, and it hit me. Sitting alone in my office, the lightbulb went on, and I got it. I freaking got it! I wanted to call Marty to tell him that I finally understood what he meant. When you are the top person in an organization, you can no longer point to someone above you and shift responsibility. That means that every decision is yours and yours alone, and even if you've collected other opinions and data and made an informed decision, it's still not going to please everyone.

Even with the best of intentions, a leader is going to upset someone. Whether it be through a policy decision, a choice for promotion, or administering discipline, leaders disappoint people. Even when attempting to implement something new and big that will change an organization for the better, people resist because it's different from what they are used to. People are creatures of habit, and they don't particularly like to be forced out of their comfort zones, and when their environment shifts, they stand their ground in defense of it.

I had only been the chief for one year in my organization when I became conscious of all the people I had already disappointed. Even though I believed I could see things so clearly that needed to be changed or people that needed to be disciplined, others did not agree.

Marty was right. Being a leader who actually transforms an organization invariably means that some people are going to get left behind. It also means that you have to find the precise amount of transformation because people who walk in and decide to scrap everything are making a mistake. Every organization has a lot of wonderful in it, and those things should be left exactly as they are. But the things that need to be changed should be changed even if it means that people are disappointed in the process. I have found that it's the transitional part of change that people cannot tolerate. But once you get through the part of change that's uncomfortable and you get to the other side, people are appreciative and even wonder why we didn't do it sooner. If you are comfortable with making others uncomfortable, you can transform an organization. Sometimes we need to blow up the template of what we've always done to begin a transformation. And that might mean making others uncomfortable in the process.

At my swearing-in as chief, I made a promise to the police officers in my department that I would ask myself three questions before making a decision: 1) Am I doing the right thing, 2) at the right time, and 3) for the right reasons? I vowed that if I ever answered "no" to any of those questions, I would not proceed. But if the answer was affirmative to all, I would move forward unapologetically.

So carry on in disappointing people, but make sure it's at the rate they can absorb.

WHEN THE STUDENT IS READY, THE MASTER APPEARS

When I was a nineteen-year-old cadet, a captain in my police department took a professional interest in me. Michael Nila took me under his wing and pushed me so hard that I don't believe I would have been promoted through the ranks had it not been for his influence. I didn't have a clue back then, but as I retrace my steps, I realize the impact he had on my success. Captain Nila was a tough cop in his day, but he was also an academic cop before it was cool. He told me stories of how the other officers had porn magazines stashed in their desk drawers while he had leadership books. His intellect and drive made him the youngest officer ever promoted to sergeant and then to lieutenant, and he believed people resented him for that. When his boss called him into the office to ask him not to bring books to the department, he started carrying a briefcase with his academic literature so no one could see it. Problem solved. I found it hilarious that he had to smuggle leadership books to and from work. It speaks to the old culture of policing and lends itself to the level of anti-intellectualism our profession once had.

Michael made lieutenant and captain in his early forties, so it seemed pretty clear to me that he was doing something right. Captain Nila changed me for the better. He pushed me toward education, and he insisted that I take my career into my own hands.

One night at work, he handed me a flyer and strongly suggested that I attend an event in Chicago where author Stephen Covey would be lecturing on his book *The 7 Habits of Highly Effective People*. The event was on my day off, and I recalled having a fleeting thought about spending my off time in a lecture listening to a guy I'd never heard of, but I also didn't want to disappoint my boss—so I went. I remember sitting in the audience being fully conscious of the exact moment all the molecules inside me shifted. I was in the front row, and Covey was lecturing on each of the seven leadership habits, and that's when I became enlightened to the roadmap for success. The principles Covey taught were universal, and they became ingrained in the way I did my job from that moment forward. By adopting the second habit— to "begin with the end in mind"—I drafted my blueprint for the path forward. Each habit built upon the last, and when I adhered to them, success was the natural consequence.

Captain Nila exposed me to an academic world I didn't know existed. I suddenly understood why he pursued knowledge, because even though it had nothing to do with policing, it had everything to do with policing. Before that time, I had only read cop books because it seemed obvious that's what I should do. But when I started branching out into leadership and the psychology of people, it changed the way I saw the world. I began reading everything I could get my hands on. Captain Nila delved even deeper into Covey's material and decided to pursue his certification to teach for Stephen Covey's company, Franklin Covey. The certification required learning the material and following a set curriculum to teach it. Once he got proficient at instructing, he encouraged me to do the same. I was reluctant to begin teaching because I didn't feel as though I had successfully mastered the seven habits. Habit #5—to "seek first to understand, and then be understood"—tripped me up a lot because in my twenties, my default was to skip the part where I tried to understand and get to the part where I was understood. I was impatient and still found myself resorting to my bossy self. I called Michael one day and told him I couldn't teach the seven habits to others because I was stumbling over them myself. It seemed hypocritical to teach on matters of enlightenment when I was far from it.

The answer came from Stephen Covey himself—not in a dream or anything weird like that. Michael had called Covey, who responded that even he struggled with following all the habits all the time. Indeed, the journey is in the struggle, and being conscious of falling off the path is part of the process to get back on it. There you have it. Stephen said it was okay that I wasn't perfect, so I pressed on and got better and better at recognizing when I wasn't in alignment. The more I taught, the better I understood the habits, and the better I got at applying them. It was the most defining time in my life because it set me on a trajectory to commit myself to constant self-improvement.

I started to find my voice, and I applied everything I was learning in my role as a cop. I got better at my job because of it. Captain Nila retired in 1999, so I had only five years on the job when he left, but his influence on me didn't stop when he left the police department. Nila trained me to branch out in my teaching, and I taught diversity and leadership classes on my days off, traveling to police departments and organizations all over the nation. Although I was in the instructor role, I learned more from the class participants and my co-facilitators than they did from me.

After I was promoted to sergeant, Nila suggested I go back to school to earn my master's degree. Then he steered me toward a leadership program at Harvard. My police department didn't have the budget to send me to the Harvard Kennedy School, so he encouraged me to apply for a grant from a private foundation. He made me understand that there was always a way through even if it wasn't a straight line.

I've tried to pay it forward by identifying officers who possess talent and passion. When someone exhibits "boss" qualities, tell them. It costs you nothing, and it doesn't diminish you in any way. And if you are on the receiving end of a person who tells you they see a spark of greatness in you, listen to them. Good leaders see those sparks, and the best leaders help you turn that spark into a burning inferno. Listen to them and let them guide you. It's been my experience that the people who have potential rarely see it in themselves. That's the paradox of being amazing. If you truly are, you don't know it.

This book is the result of my high school English teacher, Barb Blom. I had her for creative writing my junior year, and one day as class was being dismissed, she pulled me aside and asked me to join the newspaper staff. She was the advisor to the school paper and told me she liked my writing and thought I'd be good at it. I wasn't a great student, but her class was the only one I enjoyed. I was elated that she took notice of my writing, and I accepted her offer. I became an editor of the newspaper, but what changed my trajectory was Barb giving me my own editorial column called "Straight from the Heart." It was cheesy and idealistic, but it set the course for the editorial column on policing I would later have in the *Chicago Tribune Beacon-News*. That carved the path for my blog and, eventually, this book. Barb Blom identified a talent that was invisible to me, and I am forever grateful to her for awakening my passion for the written word.

If you have accomplished something in your life, chances are many people helped you get there. Even though we feel grateful, we hardly ever express it. Think purposefully about your team of supporters and tell them how they influenced you. Even if it was in some small way, they would appreciate knowing that they were one of the people who saw something in you that you didn't see in yourself.

As previously described in the "Tormentor" chapter, some people with power view everyone as competition and use their authority to keep others down because they feel threatened by talent. Fortunately, other people with power don't feel as though helping to elevate someone else strips them of their power. They understand that talent is abundant if you take the time to cultivate it. They are the kind of people who move an organization onward and upward.

Your job is to look for opportunities to better those around you by recognizing what gifts and talents they possess. When you see a person who is a diamond in the rough, tell them what you see in them and help them to see it as well. I promise that lifting up others will not knock you down or diminish you in any way.

Quite the contrary. A rising tide lifts all boats, so the better our people, the better our organization. Becoming a boss is a paradox in that it really isn't about you. Being a boss is about recognizing your own limitations and empowering others around you. Leadership is overrated, and anyone at the top of the organization who believes he is the reason for the organization's success simply doesn't get it.

Becoming a boss has also made me understand that I need to hear hard truths. Like most people, I like being around those who share my political and social views because it feels warm and tingly when everyone agrees with everything I think. We are creatures of comfort, and conflict is uncomfortable. Asking someone for advice works in the same way. On the one hand, we usually seek out people who will give us the answers we want, to validate our conclusions. On the other hand, we can usually tell when someone asking for advice doesn't actually want our opinion. When this happens to me, I ask, "Do you want me to tell you what you want to hear, or do you want me to tell you the truth?" This one question is so powerful that it makes people stop and think. They almost always shift their eyes upward to their brain as if engaged in a genuine conversation with themselves, pondering the answer.

This is where it helps to have introspection that lends itself to honest self-awareness. Some people think on it and conclude they aren't ready to hear the truth, so they opt for what they want to hear. This is always the path of least resistance for both of us because telling people what they want to hear is easy. Just parrot what they say, and they walk away feeling as though you're the smartest person in the world. Of course, you aren't really smart— you're just appealing to the ego fueled by validated beliefs. The ones who opt for the truth after honest contemplation are the ones ready to receive it. They are the people who listen with an open mind and prepare themselves for being challenged. This is where shit gets real.

We all can see everyone else's problems and solutions so clearly. When I worked as a domestic violence detective, it was easy for me to look at a victim of abuse and tell her the relationship was harmful. When emotion is removed from a scenario, the answer is usually pretty clear, but rarely is emotion absent from our relationships and life decisions. That's why we can feasibly make a mess of our own lives while simultaneously pointing out what's wrong in others'. Our own lives are blurry with emotion, and we have to create and surround ourselves with a team of truth-tellers who will lovingly and gently sift through the grain and the chaff to expose the truth to us. It's not easy, but it's necessary.

There is nothing easy about accepting the truth about yourself or your circumstances when you're convinced you're right. When the tables are turned, I typically stay in the denial mindset longer than I care to admit. I'll fight like hell to cling to my mindset, and I turn irrational in the process. Don't bother trying to tell me the truth because I will poke holes in your argument in a feat of self-preservation. When I get into my irrational space, little can be done from the outside to drag me out of it. That's when I'm in the tell-me-what-I-want-to-hear mode. But when I'm finally ready to emerge, I will seek out the truth. For me, this reawakening usually comes after one sleep cycle because daylight seems to deliver much-needed clarity. And because I'm stubborn, I might even retreat back into my warm and cozy irrational space after someone tells me the truth. I process things in solitude and eventually find clarity in introspection, but I need that nudge from my team of truth-tellers to call me on my bullshit. Over my years in law enforcement, I've gotten pretty good at listening to hard truths because I have built a team of people around me who have the best interest of the organization in mind.

There is a stark difference between those who are judging or criticizing you and those who are challenging you in a productive way. The latter doesn't feel attacking or hurtful. Surround yourself with people who push back and challenge you when you are ratio-nalizing your beliefs or actions. You will quickly recognize these people because they make you want to be better, and they cele-brate your achievements. Those with ulterior motives will reveal themselves in time through their actions and pattern of self-in-terest. Both in your personal life and career, your truth-tellers are valuable because improvement is born from discomfort—which means you must create a safe environment for people to tell you the hard truths. The way to do that is to seek feedback relent-lessly. People are often apprehensive about offering criticism and might hold back, so your response to the hard truths could deter-mine whether someone ever delivers such honesty again. There are some people who punish those who criticize them, and that's the perfect way to teach subordinates, colleagues, or friends to keep their mouths shut. But I have tried to remain completely open to feedback even if I disagree with it. The best conversa-tions in my life have been the result of honest, critical feedback from people I respect.

In the corporate world, a new CEO or executive-level leader commonly brings a team with them. In policing, that is almost unheard of because, typically, the only appointed leadership is the chief and deputy chief positions. That means a new chief is stuck with the current command staff in place. I've always found this illogical because the new chief faces an uphill battle to convince his or her staff to support the mission. Add in the loyalties to whoever didn't get the chief's position, and you have a recipe for sabotage.

A series of retirements and events that unfolded offered me a unique opportunity to build my team of truth-tellers purposefully. Lieutenant Keefe Jackson—who I believed would have made a great chief and would have likely gotten the job had he pursued it—was slated to retire, but I asked him to stay and be my deputy chief. While he had already had a lengthy career in the military and was retirement eligible, he agreed to delay his plans to help me change the culture of our police department. Keefe is everything I'm not. He was a finance major, and I believe I was born without the math chromosome. He was a military officer, and he could see things operationally and tactically that I couldn't. His calm and steady demeanor complimented my high energy and impatience.

I chose Keith Cross as the patrol commander because he was born and raised in Aurora, his strength was in community engagement, and I knew he would align with the mission of building relationships. When I'd say something snarky, Keith, with his tall presence and deep voice, would take over: "What she means is . . ." He'd reformat my previous comment and make it smooth. He also had the biggest heart of anyone I'd ever met. He was forgiving and kind, and just being around him made me feel warm and fuzzy.

Mike Doerzaph was brought on as the administrative commander because his mind worked like a machine, and he argued about everything. Because he was a master at dissent, and we didn't see anything the same way, I needed him on the team. Mike was smarter than I and funny to boot—like stand-up comedian funny. His impressions of things and people were so spot-on that I'd find myself laughing even when he'd left the room.

Everyone assumed I would promote one of my best friends to commander. Jack Fichtel was the best man in my wedding to Matt, and he's my daughter's godfather. I consider him part of my family. Yet I didn't elevate him to the position when I became chief. Jack was the man who could write and recite policy in his sleep. When I had an idea about something I wanted to implement, which was often, his mind would go on a journey of risk assessment and return to predict impending obstacles as we geared up to execute the policy. Everyone assumed he would be chosen because of our friendship and because that's how promotions had been made in the past, so it was a big upset in the department when I didn't bring him on the command staff. I loved and trusted him the most out of anyone, but I knew I needed Keefe, Mike, and Keith right away to fill my weaknesses. I worried Jack would be upset, and telling him he wasn't getting promoted was harder on me than it was on him. He ended up consoling me. He said he understood, and he continued to be awesome in his role as the Special Operations Group lieutenant. A year later, I brought him up because he was the best pick.

All of these men are everything I'm not, so our team transformed a police department in three years. We overhauled antiquated policy. We changed our response to crime, focusing on problem-solving rather than policing by saturation. We focused on the health and wellness of our officers and provided peer-support teams, so they had an outlet to ask for help if they needed it. We launched a real-time crime center and made community engagement the number-one priority in our agency. We stopped punishing or shaming officers into writing tickets and making arrests because we understood that enforcement without being focused on a problem we are trying to solve doesn't create good outcomes. We all embraced change and the understanding that traditional ways of thinking were an impediment to progress. They all were risk-takers (with Jack keeping us between the solid yellow lines of policy), and we implemented change in operations, processes, and mindsets. We moved away from the autocratic methods of our predecessors and encouraged dissent and creativity. My mantra for our department became "The best idea wins," and we didn't care whose idea it was.

It would have been easy to promote my friends to my command staff because it would have been comfortable, but I wanted to be challenged on my decisions, and I wanted to build a team of people who had what I lacked. Promoting those with competency and diversity of thought was my aim, so I picked the best of the best to accomplish that goal. The natural consequence was that two of my choices happened to be African American. I got accolades for racially diversifying the command staff, but the truth is, they were chosen because they were the best and not based on the color of their skin. The cream always rises to the top, but if you choose only to promote in your own likeness, you will be overlooking talent. Those with skill and competency reveal themselves. My team became my truth-tellers by challenging me and one another, sometimes making my head hurt with the abundance of respectful dissent in our morning meetings. But that passion to get it right made us all the better.

The organization that encourages respectful dissent and diversity of thought as part of its culture is the organization that flourishes. While leaders should set the vision and mission, they should encourage people to use their individual uniqueness to align to the goals.

CHAPTER EIGHTEEN

RESPECT IS THE SECRET SAUCE

I am a perpetual student of leadership, and I'm constantly watching, reading, and gathering the latest and greatest philosophies on what motivates and inspires others. As I often say, I have learned what not to do by watching poor leadership and have concluded that great leaders absorb heat while poor leaders deflect it. The latter rule by fear and assign blame to others.

The question of whether leaders should be loved or feared has been debated over the years. Some believe that fear is a motivator, as people who are left to their own devices will not perform without the threat of discipline or punishment. Instilling fear, then, is a motivator unto itself. The fearful leader rules with an iron fist, achieving order through the genuine belief among his subordinates that discomfort will result should they not perform.

Even police officers not in formal leadership positions can sometimes fall back on their position of authority and use their badge
to motivate through fear. Parents do this by using the "because I
said so" approach. Anyone in a position of power has the authority
to instill fear into their people. The problem with being feared is
that people don't develop intrinsic motivation to perform. When
people perform out of fear, they soon become resentful, which
results in a revolt against authority over time. Anytime a boss
instills fear when she could have used influence, defiance is the
result. You can buy a person's back, but you cannot buy their heart.
Quite simply, I can force someone to do what I want by threat of
punishment (fear) and that method will be effective, but only in
the short term. I have worked for bosses whom I genuinely feared,
and although I got the work done, I resented them. I was afraid of
being disciplined, so I performed.

On the opposite end of the spectrum is the leader who is
loved. This leader gains the admiration of their people based on
affection. This leader typically craves being looked upon favorably
by those they lead. A beloved leader may become so accustomed
to the feeling of admiration that it clouds their thinking. It feels
good to be loved, and it's easy to get caught up in the warm and
fuzzy embrace of positive emotion. As a result, the beloved leader
might make decisions based on the need to hold onto that feeling
and, thus, appease their people rather than risk upsetting them.
The consequence is that such loved leaders will turn to others to
make the tough decisions, so they don't have to be the "bad guys."

I disagree with those who claim leaders should be both
loved and feared. They should be neither. Rather, they should be
respected. Respect is born out of high regard, elicited by a person's

abilities, qualities, and achievements. It is an esteemed reverence for skill while simultaneously honoring them for their contribution to the organization. Respected leaders follow a simple formula when making any decision—whether it be about policy or personnel: am I doing the right thing, at the right time, and for the right reasons? If the answer to any component of this question is no, the leader should reevaluate the situation and formulate a response that is in proper alignment.

A respected leader will always be transparent about his reasons for making a decision and never feel ambushed or insulted when asked to justify choices. A respected leader understands that he will not please everyone all of the time and makes peace with that concept because he has followed the formula.

When the heart is fully engaged and people believe that they are valued and respected, they will perform because their purpose and passion persuade them to do so. Think of the great bosses or teachers you have had in your life, and determine what traits they had that made them great. For me, it was the bosses who took the time to build an environment where values and expectations were communicated clearly and where I genuinely felt appreciated. This is no easy feat because it requires honest and open dialogue and transparent policies with constant communication.

The extremes of leadership styles suggest that work performance and job satisfaction hinge on who our boss happens to be, so perhaps we shouldn't focus on the leaders at all. Maybe the answer is finding the "why" in what we do so that we perform not for some*one* but for some*thing* bigger than ourselves.

PURPOSE

In his book *Drive*, Daniel Pink says that people want autonomy, mastery, and purpose in their careers. No matter what the profession, people desperately want the freedom from a micromanaging boss looking over their shoulders. They want to do their jobs independently with the freedom to be creative. They want mastery. That is, they want to learn their craft and do it with excellence. Most people want to be skillful and competent, and they want to get better and better. The road to mastery is made of dedication and sweat, and we feel great when we've done a job well. When I hear officers say, "I believe I'm a good cop," I can feel the pride emanating from them. That is what mastery feels like.

People also want to believe that what they do matters. Purpose is the feeling that their profession and their role in their organization contribute to the greater good. While at my local grocery store, I noticed the checkout guy was bubbly and engaged with each customer in conversation in a way I'd never seen before. When it was my turn in line, I asked him if this was how he always interacted with the customers. He told me he loved asking about a person's day, and his goal was to make every person who came to his register smile. For him, scanning groceries was not mundane or repetitive. Instead, he believed his job was to make his customers' day a little better than it was before they came into the store.

This is where most employees have the biggest disconnect. They view their jobs as something they have to do, so they can do what they want to do. Their jobs pay the bills, so they can fulfill their passion when they aren't working. I work more than forty hours per week, and I love reading books quietly on the weekends and riding my Peloton. I haven't found anyone who will pay me to do either. The luckiest people in the world get paid to do what they love. If you are a passionate songwriter and you get paid for your work, you are winning at life. The idea that we must find our purpose is wonderful, but I sometimes wonder if we are misguided. It seems to me that we should figure out how best we can contribute to the world with our talents. Maybe our goals should be less about seeking and finding our personal passion and more about discovering what skills we possess to make the world better.

Purpose and contribution are relatives, but like cousins removed. I read a story about a postal worker who demonstrates the concept of purpose. The job of a postal worker is exactly what you'd expect: sort the mail, bundle the mail, and then deliver the mail to hundreds of mailboxes a day. Some might view this work as mundane, but this postal worker didn't view her job that way at all. She believed that every time she put a letter in the mailbox, she was connecting people from around the world. Because of her, people could communicate with one another through cards and letters. Rather than viewing her job as a chore, she viewed it as something much more. And when you feel you are contributing to something bigger than yourself, you are aligned to a purpose. Feeling a sense of purpose in your life creates job and life satisfaction.

A police officer could easily fall into the mindset that the job is about how many tickets one writes and how many arrests one makes. It doesn't help if the officer works for an organization that values stats more than people. In going from call to call and interacting with people on their worst day, officers might begin to believe that all of humanity is broken and there is nothing they can do to fix it. Bad guy commits crime, bad guy gets arrested, bad guy gets out of jail, bad guy commits crime again. Repeat. It can often feel like pushing a boulder up a hill every day only to have it come rolling back down.

Purpose-driven individuals see themselves much differently. When they write a speeding ticket, they explain to the driver that speeding causes crashes and although the ticket is hard on the pocketbook, it might be the very thing that causes you to slow down and saves you from an accident. They are able to see that the arrests they make and the investigations they pour their souls into contribute to the fight between good and evil. Nearly every crime has a victim who suffered because of it, so arresting the offender is one of the most noble things one can do to contribute to the greater good. If every officer saw themselves as guardians for a good purpose, they would feel better about themselves and their chosen profession.

Those in leadership positions should remind their people that what they do is important, as well as look for those individuals who align with purpose—they are easy to spot. More importantly, leaders need to give people permission to work autonomously but know when to step in and offer guidance. They also need to create a culture where their people have opportunities to better themselves and become masters at their job. Most importantly, every single one of us must determine how we can use the skills that have been gifted to us to make the world a better place. I don't care what you call it but you should definitely do it.

RESPECT IS THE SECRET SAUCE

Respect is not just reserved for formal leadership positions. Respect should be given freely even to those who arguably might not be deserving of respect. Even cops tend to label those who break the law as "criminals" despite the understanding that we wouldn't want to be judged by the worst thing we've ever done. When I posted an opinion piece on my blog regarding expectations of the community on police officers, the headline aptly read, "What Do You Want from Your Police Officers?" The first comment was from a reader named Steve in Indiana: "As far as what I want from my police officers? Let's start with just saying hi. 80% of the time when I speak (always first) to an officer in public they rarely speak back or do so reluctantly."

Respect is a powerful thing. Even though it's hard to define, people know when it has been withheld from them. A blatant lack of respect is often the biggest complaint I hear from citizens against officers.

The essence of unconditional respect is to see and value others as you would have them see and value you. It means not violating or disregarding another's personhood. It means that a president of a university and a homeless person on the street deserve to be treated with the same dignity and compassion despite the disparity in their lots. We must remember that each life unfolds differently, and circumstances are sometimes beyond our control. It's easy to watch someone else make mistakes and bad decisions. Rather than judging, we might offer choices for a way forward. What's more, seeing people at their worst does not often indicate who they really are.

This is why police officers—especially—have to fight the "us versus them" mindset. Because we interact with people who break the law and know some violent criminals wish to harm us, we see the world through clouded lenses. The fact is, no human is either all good or all bad. When officers label those who break the law "criminals," they tend to withhold respect. Some officers believe that showing respect puts them at risk. Treating people with respect does not mean we let our guard down and become susceptible to harm. Respect is not trust, but it is the first step in building it. When police officers treat a person in handcuffs with empathy and compassion, I know they are operating on a higher plane and using their influence rather than relying solely on power and authority. If they have to apply physical force, they do so with restraint and out of necessity—not for the sake of projecting power.

I agree with blog commenter Steve. Everywhere I travel, I do a social experiment with the local law enforcement. I make a point to smile and say hello and gauge their response. They have no clue I'm a cop when I do this, so how they interact with me reflects on the agency as a whole. I can't tell you how many times I get the machismo "head nod" over a verbal salutation, and it makes me understand why people don't care for the police. It costs nothing to engage in a friendly salutation or pleasantries. I feel as though we police contribute in large part to the "mirrored sunglasses and attitude" persona.

This concept of respect isn't distinct to policing. In disagreements about politics or religion, people tend to default to name-calling and bullying. We live in a time when our differences result in villainizing one another rather than leaning in to understand a dissenting viewpoint. There are many topics and policies on which I disagree vehemently with my friends, colleagues, and relatives. I might not agree, but I have found that asking how a person has formulated their opinion provides me with a deeper understanding. I have come to genuinely respect views that are in direct opposition to mine when I understand how they were formulated. The interesting part about respect is that the more you give away, the more you receive. It takes great courage to show compassion and respect to everyone—especially those who look, think, and behave differently than you do. At the very least, be kind to your fellow humans and offer a smile. It costs nothing.

I surround myself with people who possess certain character traits. They encompass virtues like ambition, humor, and intelligence, but kindness sits as the highest-prized virtue. Now that I've had a chance to witness humanity through my experiences as a parent, a police officer, and, especially, a subordinate of many different leaders, I recognize how important it is to be kind to those I meet. These days, I couldn't care less about how smart you are if you aren't kind to the people around you. This lesson unfolded over my years as a police officer when I started to understand that the kinder I was to people—even when I was arresting them or writing them a ticket—the more cooperative they were with me. The more I treated people with dignity and respect (even those whose actions might arguably not deserve respect), the more respectful they were in return. This concept isn't new: treat others as you want to be treated; the more you give, the more you get; kindness is a virtue. These are life and leadership lessons that, like many, I am always a little bit surprised to find are truisms because, well . . . they're true.

Respect isn't just something we should practice on the street. A police career involves respecting the hierarchy of the chain of command within the police department. Sergeants answer to lieutenants, who answer to commanders, who answer to chiefs. From the moment we are in the academy, we are taught the importance of this hierarchy and the respect it commands. We often hear that it's imperative we respect the position or the title—but not necessarily the person in that role. That is difficult for me, especially because many leaders in my chain of command have been examples of how not to act.

As a sergeant, I set out to see if I could get certain bosses who were known for their rancor to respond to my feeble attempt at interaction. These bosses didn't acknowledge me in the hallway, so I would exaggerate a wave and not stop waving until they had no choice but to respond. At our headquarters every day, one of our lieutenants walked in and made eye contact with all the male sergeants and engaged them in conversation, but he never looked my way or responded to me. I felt invisible. At first, I thought I was imagining it, so I enlisted my male colleagues to watch carefully the next time he entered the office. I laughingly said it happened every day, and the other four guys in the room were skeptical because they'd never noticed it. The following day, the lieutenant walked in the room, and I purposely spoke to him first. As sure as I'm writing this, the lieutenant ignored me and acknowledged only the men in the room. "See!?" I exclaimed when the lieutenant walked out. My colleagues were flabbergasted that it happened as I said it did and were embarrassed that they were so oblivious to it. I felt validated, and it became a big joke among my colleagues. The truth was, it sucked. I was just as capable and contributed just as much as my male peers, but clearly our superior felt I was inferior.

Another command-level officer never turned around to look at me when I walked into his office. I literally spoke to the back of his head. I used to get really pissed off about these interactions, but then it became a game to me. For my own emotional well-being, I had to evolve from disgusted to amused. Ironically, both men had daughters, and I secretly wondered how these dads would feel if someone treated their girls the way they had treated me. I remember how all those interactions made me feel, and I vowed never to do that to another person, no matter my role or title.

I used to believe that success was defined by achievement. I admired those who achieved degrees and titles because those things seemed to be what people celebrated. The older I get, the more I have come to realize that success should not be celebrated if it was gained by harming others in the process. If you believe that *everything* is a competition and *everyone* threatens your success, you will spend your life manipulating and strategizing to keep people down. Those who make it their life's work to elevate themselves by stepping on others might succeed in obtaining power and status, but their only companion will be loneliness. In the end, titles fall away, power diminishes, and what is left is the person you are—not the position or degree you've achieved. When I leave this career, I want to say that I never intentionally harmed another human being for my own self-interest. The most important measure of success in your career or life is the way you have treated people along the way. So perhaps our greatest achievements and the legacy we leave lie in what we give instead of what we take. Kindness matters.

A basic tenet of humanity is to see—really see—another human being. When we put aside the badges and labels we wear outwardly, including titles, race, and gender, among others, we are all just human beings. Our hearts beat the same, and we all experience the same range of emotions that come with being human. I've always wondered why some people withhold kindness. Maybe it takes too much energy, or maybe they were never on the receiving end of it themselves and genuinely don't have the capacity to give it. Even so, at the very least, we should all strive to acknowledge another's existence. Looking into someone's eyes with a warm smile is unbelievably powerful, and it doesn't require words. Something so seemingly insignificant can remind us of the power of human transference (the good kind). Police officers often find themselves developing the disease of indifference because they are exhausted or drained by the evil they see in the world. The ironic part is that the cure for indifference is to begin seeing people as people—treating the person, not the label. When we stop looking up to or down on others, we foster respect in either direction.

My biggest takeaway from being the chief has been that we can build a culture of police officers who are compassionate and empathetic guardians of our city while simultaneously building warriors who run toward horrific things that no one else will. Every day, these officers respond to violence that puts them in harm's way, and recently, officers all over the world showed up during a pandemic to protect their respective cities while risking their own health to do it.

My favorite moments of being the chief were when I saw the successes of our officers and our organization. My proudest days have been when I was able to tell their stories of heroism, crime reduction, or a major case solved. While I was the face of the organization, I simply held the megaphone to tell the world their successes.

The worst days of being the chief were when I fell short as a leader and let my people down. I felt as though I failed my officers when they didn't have the riot gear they needed. When proposed reform legislation came out, some officers felt that I wasn't loud enough in protest. After the riots, my officers experienced the world turn against them, and they have not quite recovered from that. I wish I could have done something better or different to make them see how much I supported and respected them. I tried to absorb the pain, but there was too much of it.

Some of these things weren't my fault, but I'm still responsible. As I leave this profession, I will own my part in the failures, and I will constantly try to assess what I might have done differently or better. The only thing I can say for certain is that if you crack me open to reveal my heart, they will all know that even in my missteps, I never stopped caring about them or our department.

CHAPTER NINETEEN

WHERE DO WE GO FROM HERE?

POLICE REFORM

In response to the murder of George Floyd, a police reform bill passed in Illinois in the middle of the night under the cloak of darkness. I follow politics and legislation very closely—especially when it affects law enforcement—so I'm astute enough to raise an eyebrow when a bill passes so covertly. In fairness, much of the bill was common sense reform that progressive police chiefs had already put into practice, but there were some portions of the bill that would have unintended consequences for crime victims. For example, the obstruction charge was eliminated. Police reform advocates believe that charging an individual with obstruction provides the police with too much discretion. According to the new legislation, a person can no longer be arrested for resisting or obstructing a police officer, unless the underlying offense made the person subject to custodial arrest to begin with. Obstruction is typically charged when a person fails to cooperate with the officer attempting to investigate a crime. A real-life example: A police officer was following behind a vehicle on the roadway when he clearly saw a physical altercation inside the vehicle between the driver and the passenger. He was unable to determine who was punching whom but saw the fists flying. An independent witness in another vehicle called the police to report this as well. The officer made a traffic stop on the vehicle, and when he walked up to speak to the occupants, the male driver was immediately uncooperative. He provided his driver's license to the officer but refused to answer any questions regarding the altercation inside the vehicle. The female passenger was crying and obviously distraught but was also being uncooperative. It is not unusual for domestic violence victims to fail to comply with the police in front of their abuser for reasons that are obvious, so the first thing we do in these situations is separate the people involved in order to determine if anyone has been harmed. The officer couldn't determine if the female had visible injuries, but she was visibly shaken and upset. The officer ordered the male out of the car, and he refused. This is obstruction. The officer was able to charge this Class A misdemeanor. Under the reform bill, the officer could do absolutely nothing. The officer had reasonable suspicion but not probable cause for a battery arrest because neither were cooperative. So the man driving could simply refuse any commands from the officer and drive away. If you agree that no one should have to exit their car and obey commands from a police officer, you are probably satisfied with the way the scenario ends. However, let's play this out a little further. The man drives away with the female and two hours later, she's found dead. This is not an unrealistic stretch. Had the officer been able to separate them and determine what occurred, she'd still be alive. Had the officer been able to charge him with obstruction, she would still be alive. Let's say the female is your daughter or your sister, and you later learn that the officer pulled the car over hours earlier to investigate a battery. You would blame the police officer for letting them go.

I could play out another hundred scenarios for you that illustrate the same potential outcomes. It is rare that an officer stumbles upon a crime that they see being committed. It happens, but it's far more common for the police to be called by a witness or victim to a crime. The police officer then attempts to gather facts and evidence to determine the offender they suspect committed the crime. But if this suspect decides they don't want to provide identification, answer questions, or remain detained, they can walk away. Criminals become emboldened, and crime goes up. The unintended consequences are that there are more crime victims left without justice because the police can't do their job.

Another absurdity in the legislation included not allowing an officer to view their bodycam footage before writing a report. I'm not a big sports fanatic, but even I know that referees get to look at several camera angles before they make a call—and their call is not a life-or-death decision. Sorry, sporty ball fans, but it is *just a game*. Police officers are running into gunfire, chasing down carjackers and armed robbers, and attempting to stop violent offenders. The authors of this bill didn't take into consideration that an officer has seconds to make decisions to save their own life or the life of someone else. In a high-stress situation, they aren't going to be able to recall every moment of the terrifying incident precisely as it unfolded. But under this reform bill, they would be required to write their report using only their recollection. And God forbid they write something in the report that doesn't precisely align with the bodycam video. That is setting up a cop for a "gotcha," and it's preposterous.

These two reform examples are meant to stop rogue cops, and I understand the thought process behind those who proposed the legislation. I heard from the legislators themselves personal stories of being stopped by the police and charged with obstruction for failing to obey an officer's commands. And they weren't doing anything wrong. I have also seen examples of officers who manipulate and deceive by yelling "stop resisting" to a person who clearly isn't resisting. These are the fringe, and a sweeping reform bill will only serve to tie the hands of competent and honest police officers who are simply trying to determine if a crime has been committed.

Before we institute sweeping changes to laws, we must come to the table and work through these matters together. Had the legislators invited police officers to provide some insight and real-life examples of using the obstruction law for the purpose of solving crimes and protecting victims, we would have eliminated much of the uproar from the law enforcement community. We spent six months fighting this reform bill and the atrocities in it, and the lawmakers capitulated to the arguments about unintended consequences and eventually altered the bill. I believe with all my heart that the intentions of the legislators were to throw roadblocks in front of bad cops, and I agree with them wholeheartedly that we must do everything in our power to hold rogue cops accountable and push them out of our profession. But these reform measures didn't consider the honorable and noble work done every single day by officers who follow the law and use it for good.

Police officers who walk into harm's way to stop an active shooter or detain a suspect will begin to think twice if they aren't provided protections under the law. If state's attorneys and judges don't prosecute cases where a legal arrest was made, officers will stop making arrests. As police officers are vilified and the defund and abolish movements continue, good cops will begin to do the unthinkable. They will turn corners in their squad car, and they won't actively engage in enforcing the law. For those who say that is precisely what they want—for cops to stop policing, I desperately hope you are never the victim of a crime. Interestingly enough, one of the state representatives who authored the Illinois reform bill was a victim of a carjacking shortly thereafter. That does not give me any satisfaction whatsoever, but it does illustrate the problem of perspective. We believe in our own perspective so much, and we double down on our beliefs when challenged—that is, until something happens to us that offers a new perspective. When cops do their jobs justly, they should be safe and supported. I fear for a world where there are no police to safeguard the community, and it is my prediction that the pendulum will shift back to support for the police. But unfortunately, violent crime has risen. There has been a nearly 30 percent increase in murders because those harming our communities are not suffering any consequences. Police are afraid to become the next viral video (even when acting justly), so why should they intervene? It may be too simplistic to blame the rise in crime entirely on changes in policing as a result of the defund/abolish movements, but the data was clear well before the pandemic that less active policing correlates with a rise in crime rates.

CRIMINAL JUSTICE ECOSYSTEM

As I write this, the Chicago Police Department has taken a record number of guns off the street. In 2019, they seized ten thousand illegal guns. They are on track to surpass that number this year (2021). I'm not a genius, but what that means is the cops are out there doing their jobs. You would think that taking more guns off the street would result in fewer shootings. You'd be wrong. The same offenders with gun charges keep shooting. Before the Fourth of July weekend, Chicago aldermen demanded that the superintendent give them a plan on what the police were going to do. He outlined the plan of enforcement, and as I watched, I wanted him to say what we all are thinking: stop putting the onus on the police alone to stop people from shooting. When shooters keep getting low bonds from judges, and state's attorneys don't push for jail time, the result is this. Shooters are placed on electronic monitoring, and this might surprise you, but they keep shooting while on electronic monitoring. Our partners in the criminal justice system have a greater impact on outcomes than police. Why would a violent offender change their ways if they suffer no consequences? I often hear that we cannot arrest our way out of this problem, and once again, I'm only of average intelligence, but it seems to me that if shooters are locked up, they cannot keep shooting. I'm all for reducing the prison population for *nonviolent* offenders, but I am vehemently opposed to shooters being let out. You have seen the consequences, so until the rest of our criminal justice ecosystem does their part, nothing will improve.

There is yet another layer to this problem that must be confronted. The shooters who are killing people in our cities live with other people in homes with people who know what they are doing. Youths ages fifteen to twenty-four primarily make up those shooting and being shot.[*] If you take an active role in what your child is doing and with whom they are associating, it might thwart them from traveling down a destructive road. I am not going to discount the aggravating factors that contribute to the evolution of a gang member. We know that the socioeconomic status into which we are born, the geographic location, our culture, and whether we are loved or abused all play a part in who we become. There are so many reasons why our youth gravitate toward people and situations that are unhealthy. It is our job as parents, guardians, and members of the community to provide the guidance they need to keep them on the right path. It is the challenge of any parent or guardian to find the balance of structure and freedom. All this is to say that it's not just the police who should be responsible for stopping violence.

Stopping violent crime and police reform are separate but related. We don't want cops violating people's rights to seize guns and stop shootings because the ends do not justify the means. Police officers can do their jobs as reforms are made to the profession. In fact, you'd be challenged to find a police officer worth their oath who doesn't support what is being asked of law enforcement. Police training is often the first thing cut when times are fiscally challenging, but I will argue that spending the money on

---

* Jonah Newman, "Chicago spent more than $113 million on police misconduct lawsuits in 2018," *The Chicago Reporter*, March 7, 2019, chicagoreporter.com/chicago-spent-more-than-113-million-on-police-misconduct-lawsuits-in-2018.

the front end to train officers in de-escalation tactics, crisis inter-vention, communication, and implicit bias (to name only a few) will minimize wrongdoing by officers on the back end. Chicago taxpayers paid out more than $85 million to settle police miscon-duct lawsuits and an additional $28 million to outside lawyers to defend these cases. A fraction of that price tag could have been used for mandatory training. Any police department that doesn't train their officers beyond the minimum state requirements is falling short. We do not rise to the level of expectations; we fall to the level of our training.

We need more of an emphasis on officer mental health, so mandating wellness checks is the right call. The police culture has built cops who are resistant to showing emotion or asking for help. So they press on, battling their own demons, and don't realize how it manifests into their every interaction. De-escala-tion techniques should be woven into the tapestry of all police training. And mandating officers to intervene when they observe a fellow officer using excessive force is a no-brainer. Shame on police departments not doing these things that they had to be mandated in legislation.

FORGIVENESS

Legislation will fix some of the problems, but not all of them. I was recently at a law enforcement event and was socializing with a group of chiefs after our meeting. We were discussing the recent headlines of officers across the nation dishonoring the badge, and Chief Noel March from Maine pondered out loud, "You know that quote, 'I have seen the enemy and it is us'?" His question was rhetorical, and his words hung in the air, and I found myself thinking that we police are our own worst enemy at times. I cannot emphasize enough that the overwhelming majority of police officers are good, and use of force that is justified is supported. I'll never stop saying or believing this. But I understood what Chief March meant: we have to be better. For the sake of the profession, we cannot continue to make the kinds of devastating mistakes that send a ripple effect across the nation. People need to stop harming one another through senseless acts of violence, and the police must cease to harm anyone by abusing their authority.

There is not a person among us who has not been wronged or hurt by someone. Some harms are minor and unintentional and occur because of miscommunication or expectations that weren't realized. This is the kind of conflict we find ourselves in often, if not daily. Misunderstandings and disagreements are part of the human experience. That's the stuff of life. We are all trying to navigate through a messy world with other humans who have different methodologies and mindsets, so conflict is inevitable. Add temperaments and adaptability (or lack thereof), and it's a recipe for a spark to become an explosion.

Seemingly small conflicts can turn into big rifts if we aren't careful. As a police officer responding to family disputes, I have heard countless stories of people not talking for years over a minor argument. As preposterous as that feels to me, it happens so frequently, and ego is the culprit. We wait for the other person to apologize, and when they don't, brick by brick we build walls that become impenetrable.

But what about harms that go far beyond a misunderstanding or failed communication? How do we overcome the pain associated with being a victim of someone's deliberate and willful betrayal? When intimate partners break trust by being unfaithful or a member of your tribe does something they know full well will break your heart. What then?

I have been genuinely betrayed by people I thought were my friends or by those I've loved, and my default is to slam the door and move on. I have chosen not to forgive. I have even found myself plotting vengeance because I wanted them to experience the pain I was feeling. In each of these instances, I have thankfully come to my senses without a step in furtherance. I believe that living well is the best revenge, and that mantra has served myself and our family well over the years.

Some might say that certain transgressions are unforgivable, and that's true depending upon your threshold for forgiveness. Sometimes a line is drawn, and stepping over it serves as grounds for severing the relationship. Overcoming harms that break trust with our partner, family, or those in our inner circle requires the deliberate will to forgive those who have broken our hearts. The person who was wronged must make the conscious decision to forgive.

Before that can happen, there must be a sincere and compassionate apology by the person who has committed the harm. When a person acknowledges a transgression and offers that they were unequivocally wrong and asks how they can make it right, there is nothing more that can be done. The caveat is that the error must not be repeated, or the apology is null. You can't be genuinely sorry and do the same thing again. But when someone earnestly atones, forgiveness should never be withheld.

Those who can't forgive are doomed to everlasting pain because that stuff is heavy. Carrying hatred and vengeance weighs you down. You think you are in control by withholding forgiveness, but you aren't. The energy has now transferred, and the person who is sincerely sorry gets to move on with the understanding they've done all they could to right the wrong. At that point, it becomes the responsibility of the person harmed to let it go.

And if the person never reaches out to tell you they are sorry, that's okay. You can still find peace within yourself. I use it as a lesson going forward to remind myself what not to do to someone else.

When I ponder the betrayals I've experienced and start to feel the familiar anger stirring inside me, I needn't look far for perspective. Dallas police officer Amber Guyger killed an innocent man. She shot twenty-six-year-old Botham Jean in his own apartment, where he'd been watching football on TV. At the time, she was still wearing her uniform as a Dallas police officer, having just come off a double shift. Guyger said she entered Botham Jean's apartment by mistake, believing it was hers (his unit was one floor directly above Guyger's in the same building). I struggle to comprehend this entire incident, but it happened.

During the trial, Botham's brother, Brandt, gave an extraordinary response to the murderer. Brandt said, "If she is truly sorry for what she did, I forgive her and want the best for her." Then he did something inconceivable.

"I don't know if this is possible, but can I give her a hug, please?"

The two shared a hug, and the only noise in the courtroom was the sounds of sobbing.

Another time I was moved by an apology was at the International Association of Chiefs of Police (IACP) conference. The

IACP is the gold standard of law enforcement organizations, and its thirty-one thousand members represent law enforcement agencies all over the world. The IACP President, Chief Terry Cunningham, addressed the attendees of the annual conference in San Diego in 2016. I sat in the audience prepared for the typical remarks by the president that include an update on the IACP goals and the state of policing. I remember being enamored of Chief Cunningham's uniform as he spoke. I love the adornments of the Wellesley, Massachusetts, police uniform, so I was distracted momentarily. And then his words caught my attention, and I sat up straight as an arrow. He was apologizing. On behalf of police officers, he was apologizing to communities of color for historical mistreatment by law enforcement. He offered that policing is, by and large, a noble profession but has seen dark periods of enforcing legalized discrimination and denying rights of citizenship to our fellow Americans.

"We must move forward together to build a shared understanding," he said, calling the apology a first step in the process. "At the same time, those who denounce the police must also acknowledge that today's officers are not to blame for the injustices of the past."

I had an immense amount of respect for Chief Cunningham before he gave that speech. But since that moment, I worship the ground that man walks on because of the vulnerability he showed. He received a standing ovation. But some cops walked out. Some cops dropped out of the IACP because, in their minds, they didn't do anything wrong. They didn't believe that oppression throughout history was any fault of theirs and refused to pander to those who were blaming the profession for transgressions of the few.

The IACP and Chief Cunningham risked losing members and criticism from other police officers, but they did it anyway. That's what taking a stand entails: personal and professional risk. I was never prouder to be an IACP member than I was on that day.

There are three parts to an apology:

I'm sorry.

I *was wrong.*

What can I do to make it right?

If the brother of a murdered man can show grace and forgiveness for the unthinkable, so too can we. When harm is done to individuals or to the collective, we must acknowledge the pain and apologize. Even if it's not our fault, we are all responsible.

THE PATH FORWARD

The future of policing should continue its evolution, and those in the profession must reimagine a new way forward. This does not mean we are broken or ineffective—it simply means that we should constantly seek out ways to be better. We cannot raise our police officers as our supervisors raised us, because our supervisors raised us for a police force that no longer exists. The old way of thinking and doing is no longer effective. The cop who views him/herself as an enforcer and views everyone as a threat will no longer be tolerated or effective. If you believe you are suiting up for battle every time you put on your uniform, communities will not respond favorably (or at all). And we perpetuate this mindset by making recruitment videos of cops jumping fences and tackling bad guys. Show the SWAT team ramming a door or a sniper set up on a target and you will attract droves of people who are drawn only to the action part of the job. That stuff is cool, and it's necessary when the "defecation hits the oscillation," but it doesn't resemble what a cop does every day.

It is my belief that we must always be prepared for the worst because our police officers are the front line of defense for our communities. I'm in favor of having a tactical response at the ready, but those teams should be behind the scenes. Most cities operate in this way present day. Officers respond to calls and engage the community, and tactical teams are called out should the situation turn into a high-risk response.

There are better ways to police. I believe we should defund the police, but not in the literal sense. Allocating funding to social workers who can respond to calls involving a person in a mental health crisis would alleviate the pressure on the police to perform this role. The problem is that the mental health patients often turn violent, and the first time a social worker is harmed, the police will be right back to responding. I support a hybrid model. In my department, we have a team of social workers who partner with full-time Crisis Intervention Officers, and they respond together. The cops take a backseat to the social worker unless they are needed, and this method has proved successful. Every department should consider adopting this hybrid model.

Those who want to get rid of police underestimate the need for good people to confront violent offenders. Until human beings stop acting barbaric, we need the police. Period. The police officers we need are hard to find because they are a special breed. They understand that they may be called to action, and they willingly accept the risk of stepping into harm's way. They are fully prepared to sacrifice their own life to save the life of a person they have never even met. Yet they must be able to show empathy and compassion for their fellow humans. Every time they respond to a call for service, they must remember these words: "I am here to help." They must be able to problem-solve using complex and critical thinking skills to arrive at the best outcome. The modern-day police officer must encompass the courage of an ethical warrior and the heart of a guardian. These police officers exist. I know because I have seen them. I have stood shoulder to shoulder with them.

The most important lesson to take away from all of this is that we can hold simultaneous thoughts. We can support our police and still want reform that makes our police better. We can support police and still denounce cops who violate society's trust by being unfaithful to the profession. These things aren't mutually exclusive.

CONCLUSION

I have come a long way from the bar I grew up in, and I haven't stepped foot in a Long John Silver's in three decades. Despite the complexities of my childhood, I am blessed to be the product of two flawed humans who made me, and I have just now begun to understand the gifts I was given from my mother, who is incapable of seeing anything but the best in people. She softened the rough and calloused edges that my dad constructed in me. The latter built my resilience and persistence, and the former taught me to feel empathy and compassion for others. I understand now how these skills made me a better police officer and leader.

Every single one of us is made up of flaws that are stitched together to form a life. Our flaws can either weigh us down and provide an excuse as to why we cannot succeed, or they can be stepping stones to overcoming hardships and obstacles. This is true of those who have found themselves on the wrong side of the law as well as those who have been dealt a losing hand in life. Our mistakes do not define us, and we get to rewrite our narrative if we choose. The lessons I've learned in leadership and in life can be summarized in a few thoughts. When I chose to push through fear, I have never regretted it. I have failed publicly and privately, but I have failed forward. Every time I fell short, I gained knowledge and experience. Learn to fail well, and you will eventually see how much distance you have covered.

My story is as unique to me as yours is to you, and the beauty of stories is that they never end. As I walk out of the police department, I know I have left something of me behind, and I'm proud of my legacy. The only real battle I've had as of late is between hanging on and letting go. I've always loved the saying, "A lady always knows when to leave," and I think of that as I attempt to reconcile the police life I leave behind. There is a part of me that is grappling with the notion that I'm abandoning my profession during a tumultuous time, and then I remind myself that we are all replaceable when it comes to our jobs, and my department is in caring and capable hands with the team who will succeed me. I am finding strength in this moment of weakness because I'm at peace with my story. It's filled with failures and missteps, but those are what make the journey worthwhile. And I have found that my life has been a series of leaping into things for which I am not quite ready. Parenthood, marriage, and promotions are all things we enter into before knowing what to expect. With each embarkment into new territory, I've been terrified and ecstatic at the same time. The same is true now as I leave my beloved department and my hometown to embark on uncharted territory.

I have achieved success if you define success by way of titles. As I shed my title, I am left with the person I've become over my forty-eight years—thirty spent in law enforcement. We spend a great deal of our lives chasing the idea of success. When I was little, my pinnacle was becoming a cop. Then I continued to move the goalpost, and no matter what I achieved, I wanted more. I pursued another degree, I took another promotion exam, and I applied for bigger jobs. If I allow myself to believe that I have reached the summit of success as defined by society, that means I have nowhere left to climb, and that makes me feel unsettled. Fortunately, I know that's not true because I subscribe to a different definition of success. There are miles to go before I sleep, and I choose to keep climbing and contributing. I'm excited and scared.

The real fear I have is not for my own livelihood. I am afraid for my profession because it is so misunderstood. Those who feel oppressed and harmed by police officers can say the same. We are all misunderstood—individually and collectively. And the only way we can begin to heal as a nation and in our respective corner of the world is to lean into the discomfort of misunderstanding. Leaning in also means leaning into self-reflection. We cannot lean into one another without first asking if we are, ourselves, the enemy. What personal responsibility do we have in our society to protect it from harm? At first glance, that might appear to fall on the shoulders of police officers, but it doesn't. Every single one of us must play a part in keeping our own house in order. Accountability begins with the individual and then the tribe. While police have made errors that are unforgivable, the police aren't the problem, friends. Violence, no matter whose hands are inflicting it, is the problem.

I hope I have imparted the lessons I've learned and offered a glimpse into a cop's world so you can better understand it. Naturally, my perspective is my own, but the universal lessons apply to everyone. It's a bit sad that many of the lessons I've learned came from understanding what not to do from watching others, but even that is a gift if you stop and think about it. There is freedom in being able to choose how not to behave. When we experience a bad boss or are the product of a bad environment, we can choose not to repeat the same behavior. Some people use the excuse of having been treated badly as justification to do the same to others, but that won't serve you well. Knowing better means you must do better. Remembering how it felt to be on the receiving end of harm should motivate each one of us to treat people with the care we wished we'd received.

History will not look favorably on this moment in time. We are a nation divided politically, and violence in our cities is higher than it has been in a decade. We are fighting demons in the form of poverty, inequality, mental illness, substance abuse, and inhumanity. But the greatest of all these is inhumanity because if we treated people as humans, these listed conditions would be handled with care. We spend so much time focusing on the things that divide us rather than on those that unite us. Every human creature wants the same thing: to love and be loved and to provide for their tribe. We all want to be respected for our personhood, and we want not to be harmed. Whether we are pro-life or pro-choice, pro-police or anti-police, black or white, we are all living and breathing humans that deserve to move about the world in our own way. As long as we aren't harming one another, we should be free to pray to the god we choose or love the person we love. Above all, not one of us should ever believe that we are better than another. Inequity is born from the belief of feeling superior to another. We are all just trying to climb our own mountains.

You are alive at an absolutely critical moment in time. Show up for this life, and find your purpose. But don't stop there, because that only serves you. Your true calling is determining your gift and then using it to serve the world.

ACKNOWLEDGMENTS

This book wouldn't exist if it weren't for Barbara Blom. She is living proof that educators have the power to change the trajectory of a life. Barb, you will never know the depth and breadth of my gratitude for how you recognized the mediocre talent in my sixteen year old self and helped me hone it. Because of you, I worship and understand the power of words. Chance made you my teacher. Choice has made us lifelong friends.

Noel Yucuis edited my thesis for the Naval Postgraduate School, and I turned to her to help me with this project. I had no idea what I was doing, and she helped me get this work to a place where it was ready to reveal. Then, Naren Aryal from Amplify Publishing read my manuscript over a weekend and decided to take me on. Naren, I didn't look beyond you because "you know when you know." The entire team at Amplify turned this concept into a book. Thank you for making this real.

To the Fisher family and the Maberry-Eastman family, who let me freeload in their homes during my high school years. Your selflessness saved a wayward child who just wanted to be a part of a big family. Someday I intend to pay you back for the vacations and the tuna casserole.

Carrie Fisher and Dawn Batchelor are my oldest and dearest friends. Since junior high, we have ridden life's roller coaster together and, despite the lulls of contact when life was busy consuming us, I always knew we'd keep picking up where we left off. Let's keep floating around the pool together until we break our hips. Then, let's race our wheelchairs.

I was born an only child, but I know what it's like to have big brothers thanks to Keefe Jackson and Jack Fichtel. They are remarkable colleagues and, because of their talent and competency, our department got better. Keefe and Jack, I knew I could fall backward and you would catch me. I knew you would call me on my bullshit. You are the best men I've ever met.

Carol Burns, Debi Cain, Andrea Darlas, Sylvia Moir, and Celenez Nunez. You are warrior women and your contributions to your life's work inspire me. You are busy changing the world in our profession (and in the media), yet you still have time to help other women along the way. You are all a rare gift in my life. Thank you for showing me that we are here to straighten each other's crowns.

To my tormentors, from you I have learned to convert criticism to fuel, and I am so resilient because of it. You have taught me that weak people devote their lives to harm and hatred and that my best revenge is living well. What a gift.

Karie Hill-Gray, the tapestry of my life has you woven through almost all of it. Through transition and strife and laughter and love, you were foundational. Dr. Amy Avery, I found you when I was shopping online for a friend. I picked you because your grammar and spelling was impeccable in our back and forth correspondence. You both will be my family until the end of time.

Sheila Conrad and Alex Voigt were the first to lay eyes on the edited work of this book, and they offered an obnoxious amount of content suggestions that made it better. Their brutal honesty and nerdy love of the English language is one of the many reasons I adore them. Sheila and Alex, we'd been through a lot of life together before this manuscript and, now that you are in the acknowledgement, you can never leave.

Mike, Ryan, and Jurgita put up with me as I sent excerpts and constant updates on the word count. Like best friends do, they continued to encourage me to write on. You are my tribe and my lifeline, and I hope our text group chat is never muted.

My beautiful mother passed away a few short months before this book went to print. I thought I had more time to tell her that her love and pride made me into the confident woman I became. Mom, you did the very best you could. You made me kind and creative, and I didn't realize how much of your best parts found their way to me until you were gone.

Chris, my partner in love and life, proofread every sentence on every page for every revision and told me she got something new from each read. Chris, your confidence in me makes me unafraid. I am so glad I get to navigate this life with you. You are strong when I am weak, and I finally understand that it's okay to need someone. (Note to self to delete previous sentence and revert to avoiding vulnerability.) Thank you for always fighting for us and our family. Now that this book is complete, I'm bored so buckle up for our next adventure.

Bailey Ziman made me a "mother," my most valued and accomplished title. She rearranged all my molecules and I didn't think I could fit any more love in my heart until Jake Ziman came along twenty months later and showed me that love can overflow and still abound. Boo, your resilience and fierceness ensures you will succeed in anything you do. I am beyond proud that the USAF gets to utilize your talents and skills in service. Jake, you are ridiculously talented, funny, and kind, and the art you are contributing to the world is going to make it better. You both are my greatest achievement. My bonus children, Megan Tunney-Hizel and Jimmy Tunney, came into my life and reminded me that blood does not define a family. Megan is my kindred spirit, and her love of organization and planning make me secretly wonder if we share DNA. Meggie, I'm so glad the newborn babies you deliver get to meet you first when they enter the world. Jimmy is the smartest and most sensitive member of our family. JT, I adore you, and I never predicted your love of math would get me a discount on rental cars. Life is funny that way. To Michael Hizel and Finn Brutsman, the men who married our daughters: our family is better because you are a part of it. Please understand, you can't give them back. I love you all so very much, and this book is a reminder that what you desire to achieve is on the other side of action. Do what you have to do so you can do what you want to do.